THE Dream Symbol Guide

Revealing the Reality of Dreams

Robyn and Brandi Cunningham

The Dream Symbol Guide: Revealing the Reality of Dreams
Copyright 2020 by Robyn and Brandi Cunningham

All rights reserved. No part of this book may be reproduced, stored in a retrieval system, or transmitted in any form or by any means-electronic, mechanical, photocopy, recording, or otherwise-without prior written permission of the copyright owner. Names of some people in this book have been changed to protect their identity.

Scripture quotations marked NIV are taken from the Holy Bible, NEW INTERNATIONAL VERSION®, NIV® Copyright © 1973, 1978, 1984, 2011 by Biblica, Inc.® Used by permission. All rights reserved worldwide.

Scripture quotations marked "NKJV™" are taken from the New King James Version®. Copyright © 1982 by Thomas Nelson, Inc. Used by permission. All rights reserved.

All emphasis in scripture is author's own.

ISBN: 978-1-953143-00-6 (Print)

978-953143-01-3 (E-book)

Printed in the USA.

To all those who dream and long for understanding and to hear God more clearly. May this book help you on your journey into deeper intimacy with Him.

Contents

Introduction	7
Arachnids/Insects	11
Animals	17
Body Part Preface	35
Body Parts	37
Buildings and Rooms	47
Clothing	57
Colors	61
Directions	69
Food	71
Miscellaneous	75
Numbers	81
People	87
Transportation	93
Weather	97

Introduction

*M*y purpose in creating this dream symbol guide is to help you better understand some of those common symbols from your dreams. There even might be symbols that pop up in your dreams that you wonder about their meaning. This guide is designed to give you a basic understanding of different symbols and how they may be applied in the proper context of your dreams.

However, not every dream symbol may have the meaning you expect; and it may change from one dream to another. There may even be a different meaning beyond what is in this guide too. God speaks to us in many ways and He has a personal love language with each of us. In one dream, being called a baboon could be a derogatory remark about your intelligence, or to some, it could be an endearing nickname from a loved one, or it could even just be your favorite animal. It all depends on the context and perspective of the individual.

This guide is a tool. It is intended to help you, the dreamer, dismantle enemy strongholds, tear down strong arguments, and build up the kingdom of God. When this tool is properly utilized, it will destroy the work of the enemy and bring light to God's plan for your life and this world.

The most important thing to remember is that the Holy Spirit is our dream interpreter. Before anyone knew how to interpret a dream or teach others to interpret, we all depended on God to give us a right interpretation. The best way to learn how to rightly and accurately interpret a dream is through reading the Bible, praying, and spending time with God, learning to hear His voice by listening and testing each thing we hear. Despite what some may say, a person can learn to interpret dreams, even if it wasn't a gift that they were born with. If gifts from God are simply something we are born with, then we have no right to accept the salvation of Jesus Christ, because hey, "You're born saved or you aren't saved, right?" Wrong (although some denominations seem to embrace that unbiblical standpoint). No one was born saved. Even Jesus was born and had to be tempted and tried, just like we are. Ephesians 2:8 tells us that salvation is a gift from God. We offer an online course called The Reality of Dreams Course, where you can learn more about the truth of spiritual gifts. For more information about this course, visit www.firesidegrace.com.

Many people will say that the Holy Spirit should be your only teacher, and you can learn all things from Him with no need for any other teacher. Some may even go so far as to say that interpreting dreams is only something the Holy Spirit to do, and no man should or can teach it. I don't believe this is correct either. In Ephesians 4:11 it speaks of the five-fold ministry. One of the aspects of the five-fold ministry is to be a teacher. It would be safe to deduce that Paul wasn't telling people that God gave us the five-fold ministry so we could learn about earthly things or earthly revelations alone. If God only wanted us to listen to the Holy Spirit to be able to learn, then there would be no need for teachers, preachers, or prophets. God gives us all gifts so we can hear Him more clearly and teach others how to do so as well.

While Joseph was in prison, he was called upon to interpret the king's dream. His response to the king was, "Do not interpretations belong to God? Tell me your dreams" (Genesis 40:8 NIV). Joseph was 100% correct. Dream interpretations absolutely belong to God. That's why it is so crucial to have personal time with the Lord and to get to know His voice.

It is key to remember that a symbol in this *Dream Dictionary* may not mean the same thing to one person that it does to another. All the potential meanings of a dream symbol are not included in this guide. The meaning will vary from one person to another based on their culture

The Dream Symbol Guide

or because of the personal language through which God speaks to each of us individually.

For instance, your father may have a nickname for you that only he calls you by. This could represent a personal way for God to let you know that He, your Father, is speaking to you on a personal, intimate level. A monkey may symbolize a mocking spirit to one person, but to one of my friends, it is the nickname that his nieces and nephews gave him as a term of endearment. To one person, a hobbit may represent a person who doesn't want to do much in life or even a person who is adventurous, brave, or many other things. To me, however, Hobbit is the nickname I acquired as a child.

Something else to take note of, is that almost every dream symbol has both a positive context and a potentially negative context. Each definition of something may vary depending on what role that element played in your dream, or how you felt about it. Not every symbol may be identified in the Bible, but still has a meaning.

Please note that for several classes of symbols, it is important to pay attention to the geographical location that is represented by the symbol. For instance, if you dream of a Japanese beetle, it could be indicative of something that has a Japanese origin or something that is from the Southeast Pacific. Many insects are generally native to certain areas, countries, or continents. Since dreams are contextual, it's important to remember that it could just be an insect, or it may represent something spiritual. In most cases, dreams are not literal, but are symbolic.

This dream guide isn't an all-inclusive guide like your common household dictionary. It is a reference point for the most common dream symbols and what they typically mean. I hope that this guide helps you to understand the love language God has with you, and helps you to develop a closer relationship with the Father, the Son, and the Holy Spirit.

Arachnids/Insects

Ants—Wise, industrious workers; hidden laborers; a small hidden enemy that works below the surface of things, generally unseen and a pest when seen.

Bees—Good for the environment; produces honey; could represent business; stinging enemy; deadly to many; stinging words/enemy attack; working together toward a common goal; remains busy, "busy bee."

> **Note**: Bees in dreams generally represent some type of attack from the enemy. The more a bee can sting without dying, the more dangerous or persistent an attack may be. For instance, a honey bee can only sting once before it dies, whereas a wasp stings many times in a ferocious manner that may even kill a large predator such as a bear. God used hornets or bees to drive out the enemies of Israel (stings; stinging words, actions, or attacks).

Beetle—Beetles generally represent something that either destroys pests or something that destroys the nature around it. They have a hard exoskeleton, so they are not easily destroyed by their natural enemies.

Bumble Bee—Originally known as the "humble bee" because they do not normally attack humans. It simply goes about its own business unless it feels threatened. Can still represent a bee in a dream, still has the potential to sting or otherwise inflict some form of damage to you; messing things up; bumbling (such as bumbling idiot).

Butterflies—Metamorphosis, change; becoming something new. Can also represent a king or monarch. (The butterfly was the symbol of Christianity for many centuries due to its transformative nature. The Greek word for being renewed or transformed in the Bible is *metamorphoo*, which is where we derive the English word *metamorphosis*.)

Caterpillar—Something that hasn't yet gone through change, but will; infant state of metamorphosis; immature; not yet transformed. They feed on leaves (leaves may mean covering) so it might represent a new believer or someone about to shed off their old self.

Centipede/ millipede—Could just be a centipede; many feats; has many legs to stand on; a well-balanced enemy. May represent the type of opposition you face, as in a type of centurion or soldier enemy.

Cricket—A type of game that is like baseball; can be bait for fishing; sweet sounds of summer; plague.

Cicada—Destructive, emerges from the ground once every seven to thirteen years; enemy attack designed to take out leadership; feeds on the roots of trees and the leaves, representing foundational attack and attack on a covering. Could be play on words for Al-Qaeda.

Cockroach—Hidden infestation; unseen enemy; pest; scatters when a light is shined on it (much like demons, cockroaches do not like the light). They will flee when the light comes on, so that they may continue to go unnoticed and not be taken care of.

Daddy long legs—Male-type Jezebel; many legs that are long and far-reaching. Spiders typically represent occult activity; occult issue in your father's family line (Isaiah 59).

Dragonfly—Devouring spirit; will feast on other dragonflies, moths, mosquitos etc. May also represent a spirit sent by God to eliminate enemy spirits from your life.

Earwig—Play on words typically meaning to be something that crawls into your ears; a type of enemy attack designed to target your thoughts and your ability to hear in the spirit.

Flies

Different types of flies represent various attacks of the enemy. It may also represent areas of your life that are lacking where the enemy has had a stronghold. It's important to remember that dream symbols are generally contextual and what one thing means in a dream may not be the same meaning in another dream.

The Dream Symbol Guide

Identifying the subtypes of insects, such as flies, will show you what aspect of your life the enemy is attacking or what aspect is lacking. *House* generally tend to represent an area of your life that is lacking in general. Houses in the Bible commonly are references to lives or families. A housefly could indicate that there is something in your life or family that is decaying and needs to be removed or restored. A fruit fly could mean that the fruit you or someone else is producing has expired, or it needs to be cleaned up in certain areas to prevent the enemy from spawning off of it.

> **House Flies**—Nuisance; enemy attacks; feeds only on the dead flesh. Beelzebub is the lord of the flies; enemy attacking your life and family; where there are flies, there is death and decay.
>
> **Fruit Flies/gnats**—Same as flies, however specifically feeds off rotting fruit. Can indicate that a person's fruit is no good and it is allowing enemy spirits to reproduce rather than producing the fruit of the spirit (which will never rot and the enemy cannot feed on). Gnats may also be things that swarm and create a nuisance, but are easily destroyed.
>
> **Horse Flies**—Powerful enemy attack; can sting. Much larger and more durable than the average house flies.
>
> **Firefly**—Can represent childhood memories; highlighting issues (negative) self-illumination. The chemical produced by the insect is called luciferan/luciferse. In Latin, *Lucifer* means light. In our modern vernacular it may also represent the light of Lucifer/ Satan.

Flea—Play on the words *to flee*; an enemy attack that creates constant irritation.

Grasshopper—Can represent going from one place of peace and rest to another; plague; pestilence; drought; destruction.

Grub—Play on words for food; feeds on the roots of plants. Can represent a larval, or young and undeveloped attack against leadership attack at the roots of something; it is an attack against a root issue.

June bug—Play on words for something that bugs you or is generally annoying. Also indicates a time of year or season when an enemy annoyance will arise in your life.

Japanese Beetle—Type of attack that may be caused by some Eastern type doctrine such as Shintoism or Buddhism; thought patterns or religious mindsets. Beetles are thick-shelled, therefore they are well protected and harder to eliminate.

Leech—Parasite designed to drain the blood/life from something, or someone; old-fashioned medicine; old way of doing things. Play on word for a person who leeches off you; something that is draining.

Lice—An enemy attack that is focused on attacking thoughts/way of thinking; beard lice may be attacking a man's masculinity or maturity.

Locust—Plague; devouring spirit; cacophonous noise; massive infestation; can represent confusion and chaos. When the locusts covered Egypt in Exodus 10, there were so many that they covered the land in darkness; consuming spirit; a plague that creates famine.

Maggot—Present when something is dying; feeds on dead tissue. The creature in hell that feasts on dead flesh; dark covering (Isaiah 14:11);

Mosquito—Something that is a nuisance, feeds on blood; something that carries and spreads disease; enemy attack designed to drain your life.

Moth—Destructive force that consumes clothing; a person who will be consumed; consuming spirit; easily fooled; drawn innately to the fire (possibly hellfire; possible refining fire of God). Uses the light of the Lord (sun/Son) to guide it.

Praying Mantis—An enemy spirit that seems religious (praying), yet devours those that it attracts to it; could represent a spirit of lust that will lead to death; on a positive side, it could be someone's favorite insect because it reminds them to always pray.

Scorpion—Occult-type attack; enemy pinch; stinging words. When a scorpion attacks, it first grasps its prey with its pinchers, then it tries to kill with the poison of its tail. Tail in this sense is the story, or "tale" that the enemy has made, or a lie they developed that is poisonous and able to paralyze and kill; Long life; able to survive.

Spiders

Spiders usually (but not always) represent some kind of occult activity or a Jezebel spirit. I will list a few different spiders and the possible meanings of the symbol in a dream. In the books of Job and Isaiah, spider webs are said to represent webs of lies, or traps that are sent by the enemy. God uses webs in dreams to represent a trap that has been skillfully woven by a manipulator of the occult.

> **Armed Spiders**—Type of attack that is "armed" for combat or has some form of "armament" to attack.
>
> **Black Widow**—Spirit of lust; Jezebel spirit; lures in its mate then devours it. Note: black widow's eggs will not be fertile if the father is allowed to live and is not consumed. Thus, if the spider is not allowed to feed, it cannot reproduce itself. The enemy employs a similar tactic on us by trying to lure the children of God away with their own selfish lusts/desires, then killing them in sin when they are caught up in the web. If the children of God do not feed on the Word of the Lord, they will not be able to reproduce children of God as effectively as they could if they ate the bread and drank the wine daily. Instead of feeding on God, the enemy feeds on his children and drinks their blood as a counterfeit of the Holy Communion.
>
> **Brown Recluse**—Multiple aspects of attack coming from the enemy. Brown represents compromise, false humility, lack of compassion, humanistic nature, earthliness or the carnality of man. A brown recluse can represent an attack of the enemy in regards of compromise; a lack of compassion; indulging in the lust of the flesh. *Recluse* could also be a play on words meaning to separate, to set apart from others, to isolate.
>
> **Daddy Longlegs**—Male-type Jezebel; many legs that are long and far-reaching; spiders typically represent occult activity. Can represent father issues reaching long distances.

The Dream Symbol Guide

Tarantula—Can be a pet or may be indicative of a type of occult attack or geographic origin of attack; originally believed to be the cause of hysterical behavior in the Middle Ages.

Wolf Spider—Predatory occult spirit; hunts its prey; indicative of church-oriented attack (for example, a wolf in sheep's clothing).

Weevil—play on words for evil: No table of contents entries found.

Animals

Alligator—Ancient evil; Leviathan spirit; attacks with its mouth and when in danger, defends itself with its "tale." Slanderer; gossip; big mouthed; skillful hunter; skillfully seeking out its food; lack of discernment.

Anteater—A person or spirit that uses its tongue or words to devour hidden enemy spirits. Can represent a demonic spirit that feeds on and destroys the industrious workers; specifically attacks people who are working for a group goal as functioning members of the body of Christ or any other organization.

Antelope—Antelope have highly developed senses, as a result, they can detect a predator from far away and have time to flee from danger. An antelope in a dream may represent the ability to detect danger from far off; quick and agile; thirst or desire for God. In a negative sense, it could represent that you are being preyed upon; easily caught (Isaiah 51).

Armadillo—Well armored; thick-skinned; a heightened sense of discernment. In a negative aspect in a dream, indicates that it could be easily run over (speed bump); lacking vision.

Baboon—Foolish person; could be just a baboon.

Badger—To be persistent in doing something; persecution; harassment; could represent a person who is harassing someone in a dream.

Bats—In a positive sense: heightened ability to hear; does not need to see to believe (bats use sonar to see their food in the air and do not rely on their sense of sight. Ears generally represent the ability to hear the voice of God). Negative sense: an enemy spirit that operates in darkness; flies overhead and tries to interfere with your communication with God; could potentially represent going into something blind.

The Dream Symbol Guide

Bears

Bears in general can represent a bear market (economic loss); predatory spirit that stalks its prey; may represent judgment such as when Elisha called the she bears out to maul the children; wicked ruler (Proverbs 28:15); strong sense of protection for children; growls when annoyed; spirit that stalks among leaders (trees); can be a play on words for bare, to bare, etc.

> **Brown Bear**—Spirit of compromise; a powerful spirit of humility; protector of children; powerful minister.
>
> **Polar Bear**—Religious spirit; strong faith; powerful minister who has become cold spiritually; spirit causing one to become cold spiritually; demonic spirit that attacks cold Christians or those who have become stagnant in life.
>
> **Panda Bear**—Black-and-white issue that is affecting your life; kind and gentle person; kind-hearted prophet who tends to be black and white with prophecy and doctrine.

Beavers—Hard working and industrious; damning spirit or damning activity; tears down leaders with its sharp teeth; something preventing the flow of the Holy Spirit.

Birds—Clean or unclean spirits. Identifying the colors or traits of the bird will describe the type of spirit that is being spoken of by God. (See the Colors section to understand the different aspects of colors and what they represent.)

Boa Constrictor—Can be a pet; a spirit that is squeezing the life out of someone; story that is long and restricting; a spirit of witchcraft.

Boar—Unclean spirit; being "bored"; being chased by a boar would be something in your life that is boring you to death or will bore you to death; may also represent a pig or unclean spirit; something that wants to bore into you; a spirit that digs up roots and attacks foundations; destroys fruit of the spirit and attacks your ability to operate in the ways of God; boars are nocturnal, therefore they may represent spirits operating in darkness.

The Dream Symbol Guide

Buffalo—City in New York; sports teams; gentle giant; hidden strength and power; the word *bison* can be a play on words of Hebrew word *tsibon*, meaning "hyena, wolf, robber, or iniquity that dwells."

Bull—Strength; power; stubbornness; being bull-headed; play on words for something being malarkey; an unclean spirit that attacks in anger; persecution; bull market; bulls of Bashan representing evil spirits seeking to destroy; see Psalm 22.

Cardinal—Directional; play on word for carnal; religious spirit; a shift of direction; going in a new course of action; to some, it may represent a cardinal sin; religious leader or higher authority giving you guidance.

Camel—Depending on geographic location, may represent what drives you or a means of transportation; beast of burden; not graceful; enduring. Ability to store water for long periods of time; welling up the Holy Spirit.

Cat—Independent person; family pet; spirit of witchcraft; untrainable; stealthy; sneaky; deceptive; predatory spirit that stalks its prey. Something that keeps you from having anxiety; a best friend (to some).

Cheetah—Quick predatory spirit; play on words for "cheater." Can indicate the ability to move quickly in the Spirit.

Chicken—Fear; cowardice; gossip. Can represent motherhood; baby chicks may represent defenselessness, youth, or immaturity; protector; helplessness.

Cobra—Enemy lie; enemy attack; stinging words. (A king cobra can mean an attack on the authority by authority of something or by an authority in the spirit realm.)

Cow—Provision; subsistence; poverty. (The meaning depends on what the cow is doing or looks like. Pay attention to if the cows are skinny or fat and the color of the cow. The type of cow it is will make a difference in determining what the cow represents.)

Colt—Bearing the burdens of others; play in words for cult; immature ministry or immature power; not fully developed; new ministry.

The Dream Symbol Guide

Coyote—Predatory spirit that hunts in small packs or alone and stalks its prey; persistent attack from the enemy (coyotes generally hunt anywhere from fourteen minutes to twenty-one hours over the same prey); can represent a friend, a person who is persistent in life.

Crab—Unclean spirit; play on words for a grumpy person; uneasy to approach; defends that which is theirs; quick birthing process, meaning that it will bring something into existence very quickly.

Crane—Spirit sent to lift a person; opportunity (cranes feed on what they can when they can get it); social person; social messenger (cranes tend to be very social birds); something or someone who is "craning over" something.

Crow—Unclean spirit; bad luck in some cultures; resourceful/creative; messenger spirits/spirits of provision from God. Ravens provided meat and bread for Elijah in the wilderness.

Crocodile—Leviathan spirit; a lying spirit that attacks with its mouth and defends with its "tale." Able to take out large animals by grabbing them while they are drinking water and drowning them in a death roll. Leviathan attacks will leave you feeling like your life is spiraling out of control; spiritual power and authority.

Deer—A person dear to your heart; desiring God; timid; sure-footed; graceful; elegant; swift. May indicate having the ability to walk in the spirit quickly; spiritual slumber (some deer remain bedded up to 70 hours a day); leaping for joy; a heart of worship. Depending on the type of deer, it can represent hiding on the mountain of the Lord where predators can't reach.

Dinosaurs—Outdated way of thinking; old people; ancient evil; possible Nephilim; evil; something old being brought back up that was dead for a long while.

Dog—Man's best friend; protector. Mean dogs represent enemy attacks or people who are attacking someone; unbelieving person; people in your life.

The Dream Symbol Guide

Dolphin—Play on words for purpose (porpoise). Friend to man; protection (dolphins kill sharks); intelligence; having impact in the spirit.

Donkey—Gentle person; stubborn person; a jackass; a Democrat (election time); beast of burden; carries the load of others; strong-willed; carrying burdens of others; gentle nature.

Dove—Holy Spirit; gentle spirit; monogamy; sacrifice; being timid; easily scared.

Dragon—Devil; demonic spirit; if the dragon is for God, it may represent a powerful spirit that easily invites a person to enter the all-consuming fire of God; may represent worship in the spirit; nurturing of young; antichrist.

Duck—Play on words to duck or stoop low; to avoid something or duck out; being ducky means to be calm and collected on the outside, but frantically working behind the scenes; to operate in an unseen manner in the spirit.

Eel—Play on words for "*el*" (God); stinging enemy; typically a docile person operating below or behind the scenes, but when it feels threatened will defend itself by killing with its tail (tale) which may represent using the Word of God to defend itself.

Egret—Play on words for "a regret"; type of crane. See: *Crane*.

Elephant—Wise; good memory; thick-skinned; hard to take down; very few natural predators; long pregnancy; something that needs to be addressed (elephant in the room).

Elephant Seal—*Seal* is a play on words for to "seal" something. Elephant seal is a play on words indicating that memory has been sealed; something very large in nature that has been sealed; a large issue that needs to be addressed which has been sealed away.

Emu—Representative of someone who will travel long distances to find food; indicative of a person who will seek out God at all costs; also feeds on rocks to help digest food. Feeding on a rock is symbolic of using Christ to help process the information or food that one has just taken in; to emulate.

Ewe—A female Christian; mature woman; play on words for *you*; Hebrew name *Rachael*; something that is disgusting (a play on words for "eww"); innocence; vulnerability.

Falcon—Life mate; bird of prey; predatory spirit; messenger birds used to deliver messages attached to their feet over long distances. Can indicate prophetic insight (falcons can see eight times better than humans. Far-off sight represents the prophetic ability to see into the distance or into the future. How beautiful are the feet of the messenger on the mountain who carries good news? See Isaiah 52:7.)

Ferret—Latin name means "smelly little thief"; multiple ferrets may represent business endeavors, as a group of ferrets is known as a business; can represent a family pet; could be a thieving spirit; peace, joy, and a playful spirit.

Fish—Most commonly is representative of men in the Bible. Different types of fish are indicative of the characteristics of the person who is being represented as a fish; for instance, if a person is catching a catfish, it may represent evangelizing to an independent, unruly, sneaky person, etc. Each fish has a different type of bait that works best to catch it, just as each person has a unique angle that can be approached to bring them to Jesus.

Flamingo—Can represent a type of dance; a possible spirit of lust; dancing with the world; social media; can represent monogamy; childlike faith; discerning of spirits (filter feeder); not taking what is harmful to the body.

Flycatcher—Messenger spirit sent to snatch enemy spirits out of the air; a favorite bird; moving in the spirit in what appears to be erratic patterns to the untrained eye.

Fox—Crafty; swift; cunning; predatory spirit. Different colored foxes can represent seasons or attributes (see colors for references); an attractive person.

The Dream Symbol Guide

Frog—Spirit of lust; plague; feeling "froggy;" restlessness; can represent having a hoarse throat; prophetic messenger; boldness; spirit of pride.

Gecko—gecko car insurance; can represent a spirit or person who is clingy or sticks to anything; unclean spirit; play on words for "get going."

Giraffe—Reaching high in the spirit; intercessor; can see from far up where others can't; play on words for "garafe," or scriptures/writings; stiff-necked. Can also mean sticking your neck out or putting yourself on the line for others (derived from the days of decapitation where a person would offer their head on the block to spare someone else's); self-sacrifice.

Gnu/wildebeest—A play on words *to know* or *knew*; wild beast; a person who is acting wild.

Goat—Selfish spirit; stubborn; argumentative; unhealthy diet; will eat anything even if it isn't good for it; can represent a scapegoat; something meant for sacrifice; can represent prosperity; witchcraft (God of all things).

Goose—To grab someone; aggressive person/ spirit; could be representing returning to old habits, as a goose migrates back to their same home each time it migrates; silliness "silly goose."

Gopher—Play on words to "go for" something; a person sent to get things; possibly a type of wood; can possibly represent the grace of God in preparing for things to come.

Gorilla—Type of enemy spirit that is a soldier; play on words for a type of warfare; can represent geographic area; a large thug or bouncer; slang for a large person; ape-like behavior; intimidating spirit.

Grouse—Play on words for a grouch; grounded spirit but can fly short distances; doesn't reach high in the spirit; to complain about something; expressing discontent.

Hamster—Someone who likes the limelight; not reaching your purpose or destination; going in circles; can easily fit into spaces that many can't; maneuverability in the spirit.

Hare—Play on words for "hair"; play on words for "here"; can represent fertility or rapid reproduction of something; moving with great speed.

Hedgehog—Can represent taking care of one's self; self-anointing; can be a spirit that covers itself in poison to protect itself; self-defense.

Hermit Crab—Type of person who is irritable, hard to approach, and chooses to be reclusive; someone who hides and lives in a cave, secluding themselves from others.

Heron—Play on words for "herein." May represent a spirit of evangelism; may also represent a spirit that is "praying" on or praying for new souls. May represent a spirit that preys on the souls of men, as herons generally eat fish, among other types of food.

Hippopotamus—Spirit of gluttony; can be ancient spirit of behemoth/leviathan; territorial spirit that prevents someone from entering in the spirit, they only are territorial in water which represents preventing a person from entering the sphere in influence. Can represent either the river Potamos, meaning the river of life; or horse-hippo in Greek is a horse, therefore it can represent power; powerful ministry; movement. Can also represent HIPPA to a nurse, or medical professional.

> Both words are used seventeen times in the Bible, which represents election, meaning something was decided to happen or to be present. In Hebrew, the number seventeen represents the mouth, indicating that a hippo can represent something that attacks with its words; hippos defend themselves with their mouths and bludgeon their enemy with their heads when engaged in conflict.

Horse—Power; depending on the color of the horse could represent peace, war, famine, life, or death. Can indicate conquest or spiritual warfare; may represent having a hoarse throat; ministry; what moves you.

Hummingbird—A spirit of worship; rapid movement in the spirit; prayers taking flight; feeding off the nectar of God. In Greek, *humneo* means to sing, and it is the root of our root word *hymn*; *humneo* is used four times in Greek, four being the number for creative works of God.

The Dream Symbol Guide

Hyena—Can represent laughing; a predatory spirit; scavenger spirit that comes to feed on dead and dying things; can also represent maniacal laughter or something that is sinister in nature; robbery; something that dwells; a wolf.

Iguana—Able to break off their tail to escape predators, represents an ability to lose lies or "tales" that they have been living with that enemy spirits would try to latch onto in order to devour a person; I want to; feeding on the fruits of the spirit (delighting in the Lord).

Jackal—Can represent a wolf in ancient Hebrew; predatory spirit. Jackals are opportunistic feeders and will take advantage to feed on anything available; dragon spirit; nurturing.

Jack Rabbit—Term coined by Mark Twain meaning "jackass hare," regarding its long ears and hind legs. May represent the ability to reproduce rapidly; a heightened ability to hear; can be a slang name for *John*; may represent the need to lift, or jack something up.

Jaguar—Spirit of witchcraft; fast, agile, predatory spirit that stalks its prey; the Indian name *Yaguara* means "beast that kills in one bound." May represent a car or what drives you; powerful minister in the spirit. Male jaguars kill full-grown crocodiles with ease, meaning it could represent a guardian who destroys powerful attacks against people.

Kangaroo—Can represent a spirit of offense or spirit that boxes; props itself on its "tale" to kick its enemy, "tale" representing leaning on its story or lie for strength to hurt or wound its enemy; abounding spirit.

Kipper—Play on words for *Kippur*, meaning atonement. Means "to sleep"; could be a play on words for "kidnap," or clip to steal.

Killer Whale—Powerful attack of the enemy designed to try to kill people who are operating in deep influence of God; something designed to attack large ministries. Operates behind the scenes, unseen, and undetected attacking minsters; may be a spirit assigned by God to eliminate sharks or other predatory spirits that are attacking people who are operating by the spirit of God.

The Dream Symbol Guide

Koala—Can represent a spirit of worship, in that a koala sings to defend its territory and attract a mate; may represent something preventing you from drinking from the river of life, as *koala* in aboriginal means "no drink"; something that is preventing you from drinking from the well of the Holy Spirit.

Lamb—Jesus; young Christian; sacrifice; gentleness; purity; innocence; Lamb of God; prophetic revelation; end-time symbol.

Laughing Dove—Joy of the Lord; a spirit of joy: Holy Spirit; delighting in the Spirit.

Leopard—Can represent a play on words for "leper"; a spirit of witchcraft; predatory spirit; something that cannot change its nature or outward appearance; swiftness.

Lion—God, Lion of the Tribe of Judah. Can also mean Satan; predatory spirit; adversary.

Lobster—Unapproachable person; someone who throws or lobs something at you, meaning they toss an idea at you, a word, insults, etc.

Lynx—Can be a predatory spirit; is not a fast runner, must sneak up on its prey and catch it off guard; comes from the Greek word *Leukos*, meaning "white," or "bright light." Can be a play on words for "links" or "to link."

Manatee—Play on words for "humanity"; play on words for "monetary"; can represent provision; manna; may represent laziness or slothfulness; manna from heaven; Jesus, the Manna of Life who redeemed us at the cross (T).

Mole—A person who snitches on people; a spy; in scientific terms, a mole is a large number; an animal; a spiritual attack that is undermining. In some countries it is a derogatory name for a woman; spiritual blindness.

Monitor Lizard—A watching spirit (good or bad).

The Dream Symbol Guide

Monkey—Foolishness; a bad habit, such as the "monkey on your back"; addiction; fooling around; dishonest. Some monkeys may represent someone who is stealing from you; mocking spirit.

> Note: When seeing a monkey in your dream it is important to note the geographic area that the monkey is from, its habits, its characteristics etc. monkeys can represent people or spirits that are meddling in your life.

Mountain Lion—Can represent Jesus and the mountain of the Lord; may indicate a geographic location; predatory spirit; the spirit of witchcraft; may represent an attack from one of the seven mountains (entertainment, business, religion, politics, education, or media). May also represent Satan.

Mouse—Something small that hides itself; destructive spirit at work that is hidden behind the scenes; devouring spirit; something timid; can be a family pet.

Mule—Lack of understanding; inability to reproduce; stubborn; beast of burden.

Newt—Uncleanness; something that causes defilement for a short period of time. Play on words for "nude"; could represent a shortened version of the name *Newton*; could represent a unit of force known as a Newton.

Ocelot—Play on words for "Us a-lot." Can be a predatory spirit. Ocelots live below a certain elevation, therefore if you have a dream with an ocelot in it, you can evade it by climbing higher in the spirit. The higher you elevate in the spirit of the Lord, the easier it is to evade the predators.

Octopus—Representative of a Jezebel or controlling spirit; it has its hands (tentacles) in everything; may represent a marine type-of spirit; intelligence; spineless; ruler of darkness (blue-blooded); in some cultures is a spirit of lust (Jezebel and Delilah spirit).

Opossum—Pretending to be asleep or dead; a spirit of fear. May represent being immune to venomous snakes; could represent having a great immune system or immunity to enemy attacks.

Ostrich—Hiding your head in the sand; running away from danger; acting in fear.

Otter—Something that moves easily through things of the spirit; could represent a weasel or person who is being dishonest; play on words for "other"; play on words for "Odder," or "more Odd." More than one otter may represent many "others."

Owl—Wisdom; witchcraft; government (parliament); enemy spirit; prophetic toward the future but can't see what right in front of them.

Ox/Oxen—Strength; power; may represent a sacrifice; something slow to change; stubbornness.

Parakeet—Play on words for "paraclete," which is the Greek word for "Holy Spirit"; the one who walks alongside. Parakeets are also known as budgerigars and may represent movement in the spirit; friend; ally; may also represent someone who is immovable or won't budge.

Panda—Black-and-white issue; a group of pandas is called an *embarrassment*, thus many pandas in a dream can represent an embarrassing issue. May be a play on words for "pander," which can mean to indulge or satisfy.

Panther—Typically a powerful spirit of witchcraft.

Parrot—Can represent someone who is mocking; a mocking spirit; a spirit of gossip. May represent monogamy, in that parrots mate for life. As it is derived from the French name *Pierre*, it can represent foundational issues.

Partridge—Represents Jesus, or the hen that was wounded for her people. A mother partridge will pretend to be wounded to draw predators away from her helpless nestlings; Jesus was wounded to save us from death.

The Dream Symbol Guide

Penguin—Spending time in the spirit; penguins spend seventy-five percent of their time submerged in water. Throughout the Bible, water represents the Spirit of God. Penguins may also represent a black-and-white issue; depending on the penguin it could represent being a father or parenting; penguins, like parrots, are also monogamous; a penguin could represent God, because the male penguin both hatches and raises its children.

Pig—Unclean spirit; someone who is messy; someone with a chauvinistic attitude; capitalism; defends its territory; reverting to your natural way quickly.

Peacock—To show off; to be arrogant; a peacock in a positive sense can represent a grand display designed to attract one's attention. Can represent a spirit of lust; may represent *poikilos* (Greek for "many colored") or the manifold wisdom of God; may represent prosperity; promise; or covenant.

Polar Bear—Religious spirit; strong powerful hunter; predatory spirit.

Python—Spirit of witchcraft; the spirit of Pythos; venomous words.

Rabbit—Proliferation; fruitfulness; rapidly multiplying; fertility; swiftness.

Raccoon—Heightened ability to hear God; able to unlock things for others and themselves (unless closed and locked by God); thievery. May represent a person who eats garbage or spiritual food that is not healthy; in some places raccoons are pets.

Rat—Person who snitches on someone; a destructive spirit that destroys things behind the scenes; unclean spirit. Rats feed on garbage much like a raccoon; invader; could be a family pet; depending on the number of rats in the dream, it may represent spiritual infestation.

Rattlesnake—Long tail (tale); a spirit that creates an alarming "tale" to scare someone. Snakes generally represent lies; alarming you to unforgiveness; alarming you to not approach an area. The rattle is meant to be a warning about something; lying spirit of fear; someone who is warning you; cunningness; shrewd; smart; intelligent.

The Dream Symbol Guide

Reindeer—Can represent something that drives you, much like a car; may represent a time of year (Christmas).

Rhino—From Latin, meaning "nose," may represent discernment or "knows;" can be a territorial spirit; thick-skinned. If many rhinos are present, it could represent something that is going to crash; can represent long pregnancy; in some cultures, rhino horn may represent healing or medicine.

Robin—May be a play on words for the name *Robin*; can represent a time of season, such as spring in northern United States or winter in the Southern States. May be a play on words for robbing someone or something. If your husband or wife is named Robin, it could be a representation of that person; a spirit (good or bad depending on context).

Rooster—Welcoming in the new day; a new day; a person who has settled into rest. Can also mean cockiness; arrogance; pride; protection of the hens. A cockfight may represent battling with someone or something; pride; lack of humility; protection.

Scorpion—Represents witchcraft; difficult to approach; undermining; a stinging tale that is venomous. The tail may represent a lie (tale) that it uses to kill someone spiritually; stinging words. The claws are used to hold someone in place while it attempts to deliver a death strike; may represent a curse; something that Christians have the power to tread on.

Sea Lion—The enemy or Satan; to "see a lion" may be a play on words for the prophetic seer gift; may be pointing you to "see the lion," which is Jesus; pointing a person into a deeper revelation of a prophetic gift in the Holy Spirit.

Seahorse—Powerful move in the prophetic; powerful move in the spirit; ability to adapt in the spirit; good discernment about spiritual food (A seahorse eats food through its long nose. A long nose typically represents the word *knows*, which is representative of discernment); discerning the type of spiritual food you are taking in.

Seal—To seal something; to fasten or close; God's seal of approval; to prevent from opening; may represent a special operations unit if applied to military; something undercover. May also represent a singer or person; covenant; may be referring to seals of the end times; power of protection from God.

Sheep—Followers of Jesus; to be sheepish or shy; the flock of Jesus. To a pastor, it may represent his congregation; someone in need of a shepherd; someone easily led one way or another; submission; innocence; vulnerability.

Shark—Predatory spirit; has a highly-developed sense of discernment used to detect prey from far away; feeds on living and the dead (meaning that it is just as likely to attack Christians as non-Christians); a shark-type spirit generally tends to hunt in darker times of the day so they can blend in with their environment. They will typically stalk their prey before they attack, so they size up the spiritual maturity or spiritual vulnerability of prey. The opposite of a shark spirit is a spirit of prayer. Praying in the spirit is the best means to defeat a shark spirit that has arisen in your life or revealed itself in your dreams.

Shrimp—A small person; food; unclean spirit; bottom-feeding; taking in spiritual nourishment that is not beneficial to you.

Skunk—Someone who is stinky; a person who snitches or tattles on someone; unclean spirit; can represent someone who defends themselves with a stench that emanates from their "tales"; an unclean spirit; spirit that makes its home in abandoned areas of one's life or areas that are neglected, resulting in unaddressed strongholds in a believer's life; black-and-white issue making a stink in your life or the lives of others.

Sloth—Laziness; slow person; spirit of lethargy; taking your time to accomplish a task. Can also mean determination.

Snake—Long tale; lie; a spirit of witchcraft; demon; a story with stinging words; a whisperer or slanderer; crafty; shrewd; leviathan; Charming spirit; serpent; devil; intelligence; something that is poisoning you; attack of the enemy; sorcery; divination; witchcraft; twisting spirit; twisted words.

The Dream Symbol Guide

Note: Different snakes will tell the nature or type of the lie that is being told; it will dictate what type of attack is happening. For instance, a king cobra may represent a high-level, high-powered attack that is coming against you from the higher echelons of satanic worshippers. The Hebraic word for witchcraft and for a snake, sorcerer, or charmer, etc. is likened to serpents whispering or hissing. The Hebrew words *nachash* and *lachash* are both words for a serpent and for witchcraft. In many folklores, the snake also represents a long tail. The snake was the first recipient of a curse from God in the garden of Eden.

Stork—A possible future pregnancy or something being delivered to you; represents kindness or maternal nurturing. A storks returns at an appointed time to its haunts, which could indicate patterns and cycles in life, or strongholds. If the baby is still in the womb in the dream, it means that God is still forming this thing for you and it has not been made manifest in your life yet.

Sperm Whale—Becoming impregnated with the deep things of God; birthing something new in the spirit of God; word or seed of God going out in great quantity.

Sponge—Absorbing things easily; needing to be cleaned; easily taking things in. On the flip side, it can mean something that does very little; taking something without regard for paying it back.

Sparrow—To be cared for by God; to swallow something (may be hard to swallow or something that you need to take in); can represent a curse; God's grace for mankind.

Squid—Spirit of Jezebel; controlling spirit (has its hands in everything); casts a dark shadow (ink) to protect itself; unclean spirit; can be a spirit of confusion; mental pressure; mind control; very adaptable to its environment.

Stingray—Stinging "tale"; an enemy spirit that can hide its self well; venomous "tale." In a positive context, swimming with stingrays may represent operating with a group of people who are potentially harmful but not aggressive toward you; can represent a fast-moving car or something that drives you.

Swan—Unclean spirit; transformation; gracefulness; play on words for "is one"; irresponsible; move about in a careless manner. Can also mean to operate in the spirit in calm, cool manner for everyone to see, while frantically operating in the spirit in unseen ways below the surface (not visible for others to see).

Tasmanian Devil—Spirit of chaos; unclean spirit; aggressive person; Satan.

Termite—Unseen spirit which attacks leaders. In the Bible, trees represent people. Termites burrow into trees, houses, etc., and destroy things. Termites in a house may represent enemy spirits assigned to attack your family or destroy your life; termites in a tree represent the same thing, except they are attacking a person or leader; can represent south; pointing you to the Bible verse about Teman, or Temanite.

Tiger—Spirit of witchcraft; soul-lead person; can represent a powerful minister of the spirit, both good and evil; evil spirit; predatory spirit; only attacks from behind; man-eating spirit; devouring spirit. It can be a play on words as a term of endearment, such as, "Go get 'em, tiger."

Toucan—Play on words for "two can"; great discernment; trial and testing. It eats fruit so it can indicate a spirit that feeds on the fruit of the spirit. This can be positive or negative; if it destroys the fruit, it may be an enemy spirit, but if it simply comes to enjoy the fruits, it could be a spirit from God or a person who is drawn in by the fruit you have on display.

Vampire Bat—Unclean spirit; something that drains the life from you and steals your fruit of the spirit; a spirit that creates poor fruit in your life; in some cultures, is a god of death; Satan; spiritual blindness; spirit associated with blood sacrifice; false Jesus.

Vulture—Scavenger; unclean spirit; gathering where there is death; symbolic of the spirit of death; spirit operating in black and white with no grey areas; straight forward; relying on God for provision; strong ability to operate in the spirit (strong wings); strong immunity to something.

Warthog—Type of airplane or spirit that attacks by swooping from heights; unclean spirit; (refer to pig, or hog); spirit of gluttony. Can be a play on words for "improper use of words"; digging up dirt to find something to feed on; spiritually, a warthog is anything or anyone who tries to bring up things from your past or dig up dirt in order to feast on it. Feeding indicates having a reason to stay around or something that gives unclean spirits nourishment to remain in your life.

Weasel—A snitch; someone who tattletales; breaking a promise; someone trying to get out of something or into something; maneuverability; able to get into tight places or make their way into an area with their own effort; sneaky person; to evade something.

Whale Shark—Something that has a great impact on the spirit but may be deceptive in nature. Depending on the context of the dream, may represent a large powerful movement in the Spirit that consists of filtering the words or nourishment that is brought into its body. It may also represent a completely unique movement of God, in the fact that a whale-shark's spots are as unique to them as fingerprints to a human. Long birthing process; ability to move in the spirit; ability to see in the depths of the spirit.

Wolf—Satan; enemy spirit; predatory spirit; false teacher; false minister; one who preys on the sheep of God.

Yak—To talk a lot; to throw up; can represent power; strength. In some places, it may indicate what drives you or takes you to a destination.

Zebra—Black-and-white issue; power; ministry. Ancient Romans referred to the zebra as "horse tigers" or "hippotigris," meaning a zebra may represent a very powerful minister; powerful ministerial conquest; powerful spiritual warfare.

The Dream Symbol Guide

Body Part Preface

*B*efore we delve into the many different body parts, their functions, and the spiritual context of each, I believe that it's important to go over some basics to help you rightly discern what each symbol means. As Paul says in 1 Corinthians, we are all parts of the same body of Christ. Each part not only has a physical use or purpose, but it also has a spiritual function as well.

I always recommend reading the Bible to find verses about body parts and to always remember that the context in which the body part appeared in the dream will help to determine what the it represented. There are a myriad of verses about each physical part of the body. 1 Corinthians 15:44 (NIV) tells us, "It is sown a natural body, it is raised a spiritual body. If there is a natural body, there is also a spiritual body." It is also essential to look up what the function of each part is in the natural. For instance, a liver filters out poison from the body. If you dream that you are eating a liver or learning about a liver, this may indicate that you are taking in something that is helping you to process poison or things that are harmful to the body. If you dream that you have a liver disorder or malfunction, it may indicating that you are either sick in real life or that you are having a problem discerning what is spiritual poison versus what is good and healthy for the body.

The context of the dream, or what happens in the dream, will be the third greatest tool in helping you interpret a dream symbol; the first being the Holy Spirit, and the second being the Word of God. Pay attention to what is happening; if it was a good dream and the things that happened were mainly positive, then you can use the meaning in a positive context, and vice versa. You may also take something that is negative and put a spin on it. For example, if a person has a dream that someone came along and tore their left arm off and ran away with it, that would mean that something happened where you lost your ability to operate in faith in a certain area of your life (assuming you are right-handed). The way you can spin this is by speaking out the interpretation then praying that the exact opposite will happen. You would pray that the enemy will not be able to steal your ability to operate in faith, and that you will operate in supernatural faith, and all the enemy plans will be destroyed right now so that only the pure and perfect things that God wants to come into existence in your life will happen.

I hope that this part of the *Dream Dictionary* will be of great value to you in your walk with Christ.

Body Parts

Ankle—To walk about proudly; can be a play on words for "an angle." A restricted ankle or having a chain on an ankle can represent something that is limiting a person from walking or freely moving in the Spirit.

Anus—Being stubborn; smelly; stinky; being the tail and not the head; disrespect. Can be a play on words for "a noose"; a ring; something encompassing something else such as rings of Uranus (no pun intended).

Arms—To take arms; weapons; power; strength; influence. To have a broken arm can represent an inability to operate in any of the aforementioned aspects; it may also indicate to take away support or to not aid the fatherless; outstretched arms can represent deliverance or acceptance; invitation to something. Left arm is what you have faith to do; right arm is what you have natural ability, or strength to do (may be switched if a person is naturally left-handed).

Armpit/underarm—Can represent a stinky situation; falling into a pit or trap; not well equipped; lacking in strength; lacking in power; lacking in influence; lacking in faith.

Belly/gut—Stomach; may represent the womb or giving birth; prosperity; place where the rivers of living water flow from; believed to be where people get gut reactions, or is the origin of instinctual feelings; intuition; instinct; bravery; to "belly up" to something means to accept responsibility; to sink or fail; to turn over; to die; place where you process food and digest what you have taken in spiritually; spiritual discernment.

Body—Can represent the body of Christ; temple of the Holy Spirit; living sacrifice; multiple people; physical and spiritual representation.

Brain—Ability to think; the mind; may indicate overthinking; paying attention to something; having no brain can indicate the lack of thinking clearly; a big brain can represent supernatural intelligence;

can represent your heart, psyche, or soul, or how you feel about things; knowledge; insight.

Back—To go back; your backside; ignore; reject. To turn your back on someone means to betray them. To some, it means to disrespect them. If a king turned his back to you it was symbolic of disregarding a person; may represent comfort or a lack of comfort; support. To have someone's back is to protect them, stand up for them, or aide them. God shows His back to Moses to honor him. For a person to turn their back on an enemy would be leaving them vulnerable to attack, to turn your back on conquered foes means to show no regard for them or to show them that they are no threat to you at all.

Butt—Backside; rear-end; to interject; defilement; disgrace; shame; humiliation; covering your butt is to "cover your rear."

Beard—Maturity; wisdom; understood in Hebrew to be the bridge between the mind and the heart; a long beard represents full maturity or something that has taken time to mature over the years. If you don't cut the beard but let it flow freely, it represents to open a direct flow from the ideas and philosophies of our minds and our hearts into our everyday lifestyle.

Breast-Nurturing; *El Shaddai* literally means "breasty one," or "nurturing one," or is translated as "God our provider"; provision; a dry breast represents an inability to support life; maternity; may represent lust. Breast milk would represent the Word of God for young believers or the foundations of Christianity.

Ear—Ability to hear in the Spirit; hearing; ability to listen. Not being able to hear, or deafness, would represent spiritual deafness or lacking the ability to hear God; to turn a deaf ear is to willingly choose not to hear something; could be used as a play on words for "Air."

Eye—Ability to see God; ability to see in the spirit; lamp unto the body; what you take in; trial and testing. If an eye is evil, the eye sees and the heart covets, which causes the body to transgress. In Hebrew, the word

Ayin is a combination of letters which equals 130, denoting the spiritual eye is a means of approaching God, much like a ladder.

Elbow—God's covenant; God's bow; to bow to God (*el* means "God," and *bow* represents "to bow," or "a bow"). To branch; measurement of distance (cubit) from clenched fist to the elbow; flexibility; God's gift.

Eyebrows—To browse something, as in "I browsed through the channels." Jews were not allowed to shave their eyebrows when mourning for the dead because it was a tradition that was passed on by the Egyptians in worship of their dead cats or dead ancestors. Ability to communicate or convey expression; missing an eyebrow can mean that you are not able or incapable of properly communicating your emotions to people around you; lack of eyebrows may also indicate that something in your spiritual life that once protected your ability to see is now missing.

Face—To point in a direction; to stand off against; countenance; expression; facial features; to accept. Taking something at face value is to accept it for what it says or represents without further investigation; accept; overlook; to commit an open-face sin against God.

Fingers

> **Thumb**—Represents the apostle (a play on words for opposable). It can touch on and work with every finger, or aspect of the five-fold ministry.
>
> **Pointer finger**—The prophet, or prophetic, as it points out sin or points in the direction of God, brings correction, and direction.
>
> **The middle finger**—Evangelism (It is the third in succession, and stands between the prophet and the pastor) It is the third mentioned in the description of the five-fold ministry. The longest finger that reaches out to the world and works closely with the prophet and the pastor.

Ring finger—The pastor; it represents the loving, nurturing aspect of God that is required of a pastor (in Greek it is called "the shepherd") who is leading God's flock, and the pastor is married to the church.

Pinky—Represents the teacher. It is connected with and works near the pastor, and highlights the details of the Lord's Word.

Foot—Ability to walk in the Spirit. Measurement of distance; measurement of time (twelve inches in a foot, twelve months in a year, etc.); the foundation of the body; can represent sole "soul" nature.

Feet—Measurement of distance; can be just feet; may represent someone's exploits or "feats." Feet represent a year, twelve months are in a year and twelve inches are in a foot.

Fingernail—To put your finger in something; to figure something out; reminder of the nails that went through Jesus hands; ability to scratch an itch or satisfy a craving. Identifies issues in your spiritual body (window into your well-being); driven from men; can represent covering, or protection, of each of the aspects of the five-fold ministry, colors on the nails represent different aspects about the covering that are missing, strengthened, or highlighted, etc. (see Colors chapter for more understanding of the meaning of various colors).

Gums—Chewing something over; to "gum up" or clog something; sticky; chewy.

Hair—Covering; glory. A bald head can mean shame, craziness, old age, or covenant; anointing. Can represent thoughts or way of thinking. Long hair represents the amount of time you have had a certain thought; curly hair or braided hair represents a twisted way of thinking; dyed hair represents changing the way you think about certain things (see Colors chapter for more understanding); a new haircut represents a new way of thinking of something. Dreaming of losing hair may represent losing a way of thinking about something or shame that has entered your life; lice in your hair would represent something that is attacking your thoughts or covering.

The Dream Symbol Guide

Hands—Fellowship; agreement; compassion. The left-hand can mean having faith to do something and the right hand conveys natural ability or strength to do something. To work; to be led; relationship.

Head—Covering; top of something; God; husband; spiritual authority.

Heart—How you feel about something; Greek word for *heart* is *psuche*, which refers to the mind, will, and emotions. Can be your physical heart; inner self; love; a hard heart can be unwillingness to receive from God or bitterness toward people; being soft-hearted means having a heart that is easy for God to enter; a heart that is melted like wax is a heart that has been warmed by God and has melted for Him. Character; the soul.

Jaw—To argue; to criticize; to knock out; a person's jaw; to talk too much.

Kidney—Could represent kidney in real life; Something that filters out waste and extra water. Kidney failure in a dream could indicate that a person is not getting rid of waste in their life. Healthy kidneys or recovery from kidney issues could be indicating that a person was not able to get rid of unnecessary things before, but they are able to now; may also be a play on words for "Kid Knee," which could mean having faith like a child; spiritual discerning of the body.

Knee—Prayer; submission to God; a "kneed;" strength; angle or bend; a type of joint; a meeting place; having a stiff knee may represent not being able to bend, or might indicate something that is impeding your prayer life. To take a break; rest.

Legs

    Left leg—Standing in faith; walking in faith.

    Right Leg—Standing by your own power; walking in your own power; limbs being restricted or broken may represent an inability to walk in what God has called you to, or an inability to move forward in a certain area. For instance, if your left leg is impaired, it would indicate to most people that something has impeded your ability to walk in faith in what you are doing, and vice versa. (Remember, left and right meanings can change based on whether or not a person is naturally left-handed or right-handed.)

Lip—Edge; border; lips; communication; speaking; to talk; to border; to shore; fruit of the lips; sorrow; scorn; defiance. To stick out the lip can represent pouting and sorrow; to raspberry someone with your lips is to taunt them; to read my lips can display a type of nonverbal communication that is unspoken, but implied.

Lungs—Can represent being filled with the Holy Spirit; the breath of God; life; to be able to sing.

Mouth—Accord; accordance; to say something; to come into agreement with; the word; words; repentance. Hebraic understanding of the word for *mouth* (*pey*) is that the mouth brings reality into existence; completeness; divine order;

Navel/Belly Button—Referring to the prophetic "seer gift." Play on words for "naval."

Neck—To kiss; having a hard neck or stiff neck is to be stubborn. In some cultures, to neck is to "make out" which is a form of intimacy or getting familiar, and coming into agreement; identity.

Nose—Discernment; to know; knows; knowing something; sensing something is up; sniffing out a situation.

Ovary—Fertility; femininity; giving birth to something; to be over. May be used to alert you of a medical condition in your ovary. Speaking of things to come; getting over issues.

Palms—Play on words for "Psalms"; can indicate palm fronds, which may represent provision. Eating from the palm of your hand can be a sign of great influence; can represent righteousness (Psalm 92:12);

Penis—Masculinity; power; may represent lust; someone being a jerk or stubborn; hardheaded; carnality; fleshly behavior; lusting after something. The un-erect penis can imply cowardice, impotence, no backbone, or doesn't stand up for one's self. Ability to void toxic things out of your life.

The Dream Symbol Guide

Pupil—A student; something that is being taught; ability to see. The dilated eye can represent having eyes wide open, but you can't focus on what you are seeing.

Rib—To make fun of; to jest; can represent creation; marriage; DNA; to make fun of or "rib" someone. A rib in Hebrew was actually half of Adam, therefore it could represent your spouse or a child since they are your other half and children the two "halves" of each other that made one whole human.

Scalp—Crown of the head, or glory. In the Bible, crushing the skull or stomping in the scalp (as stated in Psalms 68:21) represented having victory over enemies. Getting scalped may represent an enemy attack trying to steal your crowned glory that was given to you by God. God's covering; can indicate proximity to God, as it is the highest part of your body.

Shin—Spiritual shock absorbers, preventing harm from impactful events in life; the twenty-first letter of the Hebrew alphabet signifies grace, justice, and mercy; teeth, to devour, chew on, destroy, think about, ponder, fire, tongues of fire, sharpen, press, eat, consume. Hebrew number 21 and 300). Can mean being stripped of something.

Sole—Can just represent the bottom of your foot; spiritual journey. Sole being worn thin may represent that you are wearied from wandering too much, it may also represent operating in a soul led manner too often; may represent soul of man; thoughts; emotions; human will. In some cultures, may represent a close friend or kindred.

Skeleton—What keeps you standing; bare bones of something; death; things that someone wants to hide; lacking in the spirit; church with no power or influence from God.

Spine—Being upright. Lack of a spine denotes cowardice; bent spine can represent not walking upright in your ways; may represent a spirit of infirmity; weakness; frailty; being bent can represent lack of strength; Not standing up for yourself.

The Dream Symbol Guide

Stool (Feces)—Getting rid of waste; getting rid of excess, or getting rid of crap in your life; deliverance.

Teeth—Represents the ability to chew on, or process the Word of God or other occurrences of life. This where the term "chewing the fat" came from, meaning to talk something over. Each tooth has its own meaning. Losing teeth represents an inability to process information in a certain area of your life; losing all your teeth may represent losing the ability to process something in every area of your life.

> **Sharp Teeth**—Words of the enemy. Can also mean ability to devour; sharp ability to tear through the Word of God.
>
> **Bicuspid/Cuspids**—Being on the cusp of something or about to gain breakthrough; not being able to gain breakthrough; trial and testing. Can also refer to cussing that is causing you to lack wisdom and prevent you from processing what is a curse in your life.
>
> **Canines**—Friendship such as dogs are man's best friend; enemy attacks, loss of friendship.
>
> **Cavity**—Holes in a way of thinking; lacking in an area.
>
> **Chattering Teeth**—Gossip; slander; being cold; word curses.
>
> **Crown**—Glory of God; losing favor; losing glory; losing authority; gaining authority.
>
> **Enamel**—Covering; protection; a gift from God; mantle; in the name of "El," can represent Jesus (Emmanuel); God is with you.
>
> **Eye teeth**—Seeing in the spirit; vision; ability to process what you are seeing.
>
> **Incisors**—Decisiveness; ability to make decisions.
>
> **Molars**—An ability to mull over or think about stuff. Can also indicate lacking an ability to properly process information (premolars: ability to anticipate what the process next).
>
> **Wisdom Teeth**—Wisdom; knowledge; ability to process the Word of God with wisdom; ability to process issues in life with wisdom.

The Dream Symbol Guide

Root—The root of an issue; a cause of things; can represent getting down to the very root cause of what or why you are thinking a certain way.

Root Canal—Digging up the root of an issue.

Tongue—Speaking in a foreign language; native language; speech; edification; prayer; prayer language; communication.

Thigh—Faith; covenant. Being stabbed in the thigh is a betrayal.

Toe—Balance; to drag something behind you; foundation. Can represent an area where a certain aspect of the five-fold ministry is strong or weaker in its foundation.

Big Toe—Carrying something great with you; apostolic foundation.

Pointer Toe—Carrying a prophetic message; prophetic foundation

Index—Toe signs and wonders; pastor foundation

Ring toe—Remembering a covenant; teacher foundation

Buildings and Rooms

Amphitheater—Amplification; being heard. May represent a location of an event, such as, "at the amphitheater, there will be a concert." Being on display; being vocal; your voice will be heard and have a temporary influence.

Apartment—Something that is temporary in your life; your life now; separation; being apart from people; seclusion. It can indicate sharing something in life that is not uncommon to others, as apartments are typically located in a series of two or more living spaces in a building, indicating that others are undergoing the same thing that you are, or that they are in the same place in life as you.

Atrium—Open heaven; not being covered; growth within the confines of your life; growth for all to see; ability to receive light. Depending on the location (front, or back) it can indicate future or past events of growth, hospitality, or welcome.

Auditorium—Place where something is heard; a message being delivered. Notice what is happening in the auditorium, such as a conference, a game, or a concert, etc. This will indicate what it is that God wants you to listen to or what He needs you to hear. Can also mean a time of great influence that is short lived.

Arcade/Arches—Playing games; fooling around; a series of gateways; may represent strength and support; Covenant (arcade derives from Latin, meaning series of arches); "ade" at the end of the word denotes something that is currently happening, so it could represent arcs or covenants that are taking place on your life in a series.

Arena—The field or area you work in; a place of competition; battlefield; place of spiritual combat; spiritual warfare; work; business.

Asylum—Offering protection to someone; immunity. If it is a mental health asylum, then it may represent getting help with mental issues you are dealing with in the spirit.

Attic—Things that are from your family that are of value and have been stored away; history, past issues of the family; things that are stored away that no one knows about (not talked about and long forgotten). Finding something valuable in the attic means God is going to reveal something to you from your family line that is valuable.

Auto Repair Shop—Ministry work; fixing up things in your life; restoring what drives you; renewal and repair; restoration.

Back Porch—Things that are behind you; the past; things being brought up from your past.

Bakery—Place of preparation to serve others tasty treats; greater influence in delivering "goodies" to people; cooking something up; service to others.

Ballroom—Celebration; dancing in worship of God.

Bar—Taking an exam (bar exam); a spirit of alcoholism; gathering place; preventing access to something (barred out); to be banned from something.

Baseball Field—The field represents the area you minister or work in. How well the game is being played and the teams that you are playing for (or against) represents what is happening in the spirit or in life. Each player has a role, and they are trying to accomplish the same goal: victory over the other team. The pitcher is the one who is throwing things at you, and how you respond or react shows how well the other team's plans are working against you or for you. Hitting a home run would show that someone threw something at you, and you took off with it and, "hit it out of the park." It is a positive experience. Hitting a grounder or line ball can represent staying grounded or operating within legal limits. Hitting a double may represent double anointing or double portion. A fly ball may represent making a play at what the enemy tried to throw at you, but it may cost you an out. If the team opposing is

The Dream Symbol Guide

unable to respond, you could potentially score a base or make a move, causing someone on your team to help you accomplish your goal of getting home. You may have as many fouls as you want without there being any consequence after it reaches two strikes, but it is slippery ground and could cause a problem.

Basement—Hidden issues; foundational issues; family or generational issues in life (at the root, or foundational issue affecting your whole house, life, or family).

Bedroom—Place of intimacy and rest. A childhood bedroom would represent an issue that occurred as a child that has affected your rest or intimacy in some area.

Parent's/Family Member's/ Friend's Bedroom—Areas of family issues that affect peace, rest, or ability to be close to a person (intimacy doesn't necessarily mean intercourse, it can also mean being personal with someone).

Bookstore—Acquiring knowledge; place of provision that helps others learn; greater influence getting the Word of God to others; providing knowledge to people with a larger impact.

Brick Building—Something made with much human effort; something that is hard to penetrate; hardness of heart. "Talking to a brick wall" means that a person doesn't receive the input you have to offer; spiritual deafness; solid foundation.

Bathroom—Place of cleansing, refreshing, or preparation. What you are doing in the bathroom will determine the meaning of the restroom. Putting on makeup represents getting prepared for something; washing or showering (bath) represents getting clean of something, pooping is deliverance or getting rid of waste in your life, urinating is voiding or purging out excess in your life that is not needed.

BB-Q Pit—Something is cooking; attack the enemy is forming from the pit. A tasty meal that has been prepared a certain way for consumption may represent a specialized type of spiritual nourishment, good or bad.

Café—Place to get a quick jolt of energy from God; meeting place. It could just mean coffee; place to get refreshed and energized.

Capital Building—Governing of the state, or nation; building capital, or revenue; seat of authority over an area; a place where you will have influence over a greater area.

Car Wash—Cleaning up your ministry; cleaning up what drives you; refreshing the direction you're headed in life; refreshing ministry purpose.

Castle—Authority; fortress; royal residence; lavish lifestyle; well-fortified place in life. May represent a stronghold of the Lord or a stronghold of the enemy; a way of thinking that exalts itself over the knowledge of God; something that causes offense; living in your royal status as a Christian.

City Hall—Legalism; city going through a transition and change; something new coming to the town you are in; capital of a geographic area.

Cities—The names of cities typically represent a geographic area where something will happen. This may be a prophetic dream about something that is coming to a city. It may, however, also be the name of the city indicating an event in your life. To dream of being in Jericho may represent walls coming down, or Jerusalem may represent a time and place of peace.

Cloak Room—A place in your life that you may be trying to cloak or hide something.

Closet—Hidden issues; things that are stored away for later use (much like an attic, but more personal). May be a play on words for "close it." Prayer life; private area of life; time of preparation.

Condo—Coming together; joint rule; a time in life or ministry May indicate a temporary time of life that is costly to a person or family because Condos are typically either owned or rented as timeshares; Latin, meaning "joint sovereignty."

Convention Center—Spiritual gathering; a center of spiritual activity; great influence over many people; church gathering.

The Dream Symbol Guide

Country Store—Getting basic provisions; place of preparation; just getting by spiritually.

Courthouse—Coming judgment; seeking a judgment from the judge; laws being implemented; coming under the law; legalism.

Cellar—May represent someone trying to sell you something. See *Basement*.

Den—A get together; a habitation of something (animals, people, etc.); a private area where you can accomplish something; family gathering area. A den may represent a variety of things, depending on what the den was being using for.

Dining Room—A place of spiritual nourishment. Serving someone in a dining room represents service to people or being a servant.

Echo Chamber—A place in life where things are being repeated; a place where everything you say is resounding. Biblically, when God says something twice, He is establishing that He will do something.

Elevator—Changing position; going up or down in ministry, in life, or in the spirit; Going down can be a demotion (literal or physical); Going down may also represent backsliding in the spirit. Going sideways in an elevator would represent being stuck on a spiritual plateau, not going anywhere. Getting in an elevator and not being able to press the buttons signifies not having control of what is happening. Promotion; an elevator shooting through the roof represents God taking you beyond the limits of what you thought was possible.

Empire State Building—May represent seeing from an empirical standpoint or looking at things you control; seeing your empire; can be a geographic location you may visit. It can refer to building your own kingdom (much like Nebuchadnezzar stood atop the highest building of his kingdom and marveled at all the work he had done with his own hands); may be a play on words for the Empire State (New York); and empirical state; the state of an empire.

The Dream Symbol Guide

Farm—A place of people-vision; things stored; preparation; church; birthing place of new ministries; representing an issue with tithing; issues with church.

Front Porch—Things to come; current events.

Foundation—Foundational issues; depending on the condition of the foundation, it could be good or bad; what you stand on; the basic knowledge of the gospel.

Foyer—Entryway to a new place in life; waiting area before a transition. When in a hotel, it may represent waiting before doing something temporary in your life.

Garage—A place of rest and refreshment; storage area; covering for people or ministries; in some areas may be safe place or shelter from a storm.

Garden—A person's heart; place of peace and love; intimacy; growth.

Greenhouse—A place of growth and nurturing; a life of prosperity and peace; growing your heart; nurturing life and growth.

Gas Station—Refueling; recharging; receiving the explosive power of God. Can also refer to a place of basic provision; empowerment; place to rest for a moment, refuel, and move on; period of brief transition in the spirit.

Hotel—Temporary place or time in life that will not last long.

Hostel—A play on words for a place where you are met with hostility; a short term like a hotel; A bad attitude in a person's life.

Hallway—Transition; the longer the hallway, the longer the transition for a person to reach their next destination; twisted hallway represents unexpected twists and turns during your time of transition.

Hospital—Healing; needed Holy-Spirit intervention; a place to meet the doctor; a place to receive a diagnosis of what is ailing your spirit, soul, or body.

The Dream Symbol Guide

Igloo—Play on words for "I glue," as in "I hold things together"; a form of a house which can represent a cold heart of a person, a family that has lost its passion; can represent a geographic area such as Alaska; could indicate how thing appear externally (warm inside).

Jail—Being imprisoned by something; being a slave to something; something in your life has taken you captive.

Kitchen—Place of service in your life; place of fellowship; place of preparation; serving others; pastoral calling (preparing food/ Word of God).

Lawyers Office—Needing an advocate; a person who will spiritually advocate for you such as in prayer or approaching God for needs. If you own the lawyer's office, it could be that you have been appointed an office to advocate on someone else's behalf.

Library—A place of learning; need to get into the books of the Bible; researching something; source of information.

Mall—Place of great provision; a place where many of your needs can be met that are specific for you. Can refer to a corporate body assisting people with getting equipped for ministry; self-centered.

Master Bedroom—Authority of the house; master bedroom is a place where the head of the house goes to find intimacy with God, rest, or privacy. If someone has taken the master bedroom and it is not their room, then it is an intruder taking something that is not theirs or making room for themselves in your life in a way that is out of order; larger issue that is mastering you and your life

Mobile Home/ Trailer—Temporary time in life, it's slightly more permanent than a tent, but can still move if needed; can represent poverty; may represent a childhood home.

Mountain—Place of encountering God; mountain of God; stability; spiritual obstacle; something blocking progress; challenge; kingdom; nation; protection provided by God. Can also refer to idolatry. The name of the mountain may indicate the type of obstacle or encounter you are facing.

The Dream Symbol Guide

Movie Theater—Going to be shown something; things on display; spiritual insight; a vision; what is being shown to the people.

Observatory—Looking to heavens; looking at the times and seasons; what you are looking at or watching.

Office—A person's office or position in the body of Christ; productivity; workplace; what you operate in.

Operating Room—A place or time in your life where things are being corrected, fixed, or removed; God is operating on something; a person is operating in something.

Opera House—House of worship to the Lord; dramatic production; putting on a show.

Park—Refreshing; intimacy with God and people; being stationary or parked; God's blessing.

Parlor—A place of solitude; place of sitting and resting; place of meeting a specific need.

Patio/ Porch—Front patio refers to things that are yet to come; back patio means issues of the past.

Playground—Place childlike faith; leisure; fooling around; not being serious; enjoying life.

Post Office—Where you go to get mail; receiving something; old means of communicating with someone; outdated communication; depending on what you are doing, it will establish what you are getting or giving to someone.

Roof—Covering; protection; praise of God; highest point in your life or ministry; at the highest level in your life and family.

Room—What you make room for; rest; intimacy; privacy.

School—Training period; teaching; teaching anointing; place of learning; time of learning; something you need to learn.

Shack—Poverty; humility; lack; shacking up with someone; things becoming rundown; sin; Shadrack or Meshach.

The Dream Symbol Guide

Sewer—Removal of waste; unclean area of life; something that needs to be cleaned up or removed; something that is removing things that are not desirable; someone sewing you; the devil; slander; a person sowing (sower; sew-er) in your life.

Solarium—Great vision; place of spending time with Jesus: "Son-Light." Making room to spend time in the presence of the son.

Store—A place of refreshing; provision; setting something aside; getting what you need in the Spirit.

Stadium—Short-lived influence; a place of great influence; stage of life; running your race; work in ministry; staging something.

Stairs—Ascending; descending; promotion; demotion; portal; up or down in the spirit; steps that must be taken for a reason.

Stall—Something is stalled or not working; containment of a powerful ministry of some sort; delaying something.

Subway—Going around something; getting from one destination to the next in a "behind-the-scenes" manner, not in the open; secrecy.

Temple—Worship of God; idolatry; witchcraft; church; human body.

Tent—Temporary place in life; getting back to the basics; shortness of life; attending to something; lack of covering or protection; tenth of a portion; being attentive.

Walls—Walls of a house; areas of life that are walls; protection; strongholds; walls that need to come down; barriers.

Windows—Vision; front window: what's to come; back window: past events.

Zoo—Strange; chaotic time in life; everything is a mess; out of order; noisy; busy time in life; "zoe" life.

Clothing

Clothing is an interesting topic. I can boldly say that clothing almost always represents what you operate in or what you are operating in a spiritual sense. However, in a broader sense, clothing may represent religious strongholds, geographic areas, a call to ministry in a certain part of the world, or they can even just be clothing.

Let's look at what some common articles of clothing may mean depending on the context God has used them in a dream. Some key elements to remember when dealing with clothing is their color and quality. Items of apparel that are tattered or torn will indicate if you are finding value or maintaining that which God has given you to operate in. A misused article of clothing (or misused gift) will be indicated by a torn shirt, or floppy old shoes, etc. Wearing clothing that is too big indicates that you are trying to operate in something that is too big for you at the moment. If it is too small, that shows that you have outgrown that which you used to operate in.

Bathrobe—Coming out of a place of cleansing; exposure; not fully covered or operating in your calling.

Coat—Mantle; anointing. Someone else's coat given to you means you are operating in their anointing or mantle. A stolen coat means that your mantle has been robbed by an enemy spirit.

Coin/Change Purse—Changing your identity.

Costume—Dressing up; pretending to be something you are not; a wolf in sheep's clothing; false representation of something.

Dress Shoes—Something that is nice and is used for specific occasions, not necessarily used daily.

Flip Flops—Indecisiveness; not completely walking in what you are called to; indicating summer season; flipping from one standpoint to another; loosely moving things; loose values; shifting; like waves tossed in the ocean; going back and forth; double-mindedness.

Hand-Me Downs—Something that a person has outgrown or no longer has a use for; gifting that someone used to operate in but does not anymore; spiritual gifts that you received as an inheritance.

Hats—Talents; spiritual covering; ability to do many jobs in life.

Jeans—What you walk in that is tougher than other things; durability; what you have inherited in your genes from your family.

Joggers—Move quickly in what you are called to walk in.

Kilt—Family clothing; area of the world; cultural heritage; family lineage issue.

Pants—What you walk in; covering yourself; the ability to endure a tough situation (thick skinned in what you walk in, for example, jeans). Types of pants can represent the informal or formal workings in the spirit; desiring the things of God (panting, as a deer pants for water).

Pajamas—Spiritually asleep; not operating in your gifts or calling; an indication of a time of day if prophetic or a vision; coming out of a time of slumber; not operating in what you are called to.

Panties—For women, it is femininity; for men it is something you are doing that is not your role as a man; getting intimate; opening up in an intimate way; sharing intimate details; lust.

Parka—Cold season in life; heavy anointing or covering; geographic location; weighty mantle.

Purse—Identity; contains everything about you, your social security number, credit cards, license etc.; something of value to you.

Running Shoes—Quickly moving in something; moving forward with great speed; what you are called to walk in is accelerating quickly.

Sandals—Readiness for action; impression; injustice; social status; not operating completely in your walk with God; exposure. Not having sandals can represent slavery.

The Dream Symbol Guide

Short-Sleeved Shirt—What you will be called to operate in for a short while; unfinished with what you are called to walk in; incomplete; covering for a short period of time.

Skirt—Going around something; avoiding something; enclosure; short-term assignment that you will be walking in or operating in temporarily.

Shoes—What you walk in; can be the gospel of peace. Removal of shoes can show distress, sorrow, shame, not walking in what God called you to walk in, not walking in peace; familiarity.

Slip—Slipping up; protection undergarments. An exposed slip may be indicating exposed mistakes; protecting the intimate or private areas of your life.

Socks—Not operating in what you are called to walk in; covering of what you walk in.

Speedo—Quickly moving in the spirit of God; exposed; uncovered; operating the spirit of God.

Swimwear—Ability to move in the spirit of God; move in the Spirit without being held back or encumbered.

Tuxedo—Formal event or formal time to operate in your calling; being black and white in what you are called to operate in; being formal in your walk with God or function in the body of Christ; coming time of celebration or important situation.

Underwear—Protection of private areas of your life; clean underwear is good hygiene; dirty underwear is poor hygiene, meaning that you are not taking care to properly cover the private areas of your life or heart; vulnerability; openness; being intimate.

Uniform—Military calling; oneness; being put together properly; corporate calling; being of like mindset; military; work; school and education; may designate rank in the spirit or in life.

Wallet—Identity; favor.

Colors

Colors, like all symbols, have both a positive and a negative connotation. There are multiple and diverse colors used in the Bible to describe God's manifold wisdom and also to describe diverse disease and illnesses caused by the enemy.

It's important to note if the color is bright, or if it's muted. A bright color will be from God as He is the pure Father of lights and colors. A dark muted color will be soulish. If it is very dark, then it is from the enemy who is darkened. Note: This is the basic color spectrum. You can take any multitude of these colors and add them together to form a new color, and the meaning of that color in the dream (if not found in the Bible) will be a combination of meanings of the other primary colors.

There is a difference between a deep blue and a dark blue. Something that is deep may indicate the depths of God's knowledge, and the deep things of His Spirit. A dark blue would be indicative of depression, or hopelessness. The same is true with any color. It's commonly believed that blue represents revelation. This is what I was taught. But if you know me, you know that I can't just take something as a fact without doing the research myself. So we will begins the colors section with what I learned about the color blue.

Blue—Revelation; insight; communion; sorrow; depression; feeling of hopelessness; piety; sincerity; suppression of appetite. Several times in the Bible, blue is associated with God himself. One of the main things blue represents is walking in the ways of God. In Exodus 24:10 we see that the floor beneath God is paved from sky blue sapphire. To the untrained eye, you wouldn't think much of that, except maybe God has a gemstone floor. A floor speaks of what you walk in, or what you walk on, hence walking in the way of God. Numbers 15:38-39 (NIV) says, "Speak to the Israelites and say to them: 'Throughout the generations to come you are to make tassels on the corners of your garments, with a blue cord on each tassel. You will have these tassels to look at and so you will remember all the commands of the LORD, THAT YOU MAY OBEY THEM AND NOT PROSTITUTE YOURSELVES BY CHASING AFTER THE LUSTS OF YOUR OWN HEARTS AND EYES.'"

> Blue may also represent the presence of God, the Holy Spirit, or the deep things of God. Since we see that blue represents walking out the Word of God, or may represent the Word (Jesus) then it may be symbolic of the prophetic. The color blue is mentioned only two times in the book of revelation. This indicates that blue is also part of the revelatory spectrum.

> Any other time that blue is specifically mentioned is in the books of Moses, which shows us the revelation of God's Word and His nature, and it opens up the door for mankind to be able to get right with God and have communion. In one instance in the New Testament, the woman with the issue of blood touched the hem of Jesus' garment, which is blue in color. From this, you may deduce that blue can represent healing.

> On the other hand, the negative connotation of blue can be extrapolated from applying the opposite meaning of the color blue. Blue is depicted in common culture as sorrow, depression, sadness. In the Bible, blue is used to describe brokenness, punishment, false revelation, and sickness; not walking in the things the ways of God, violating the Word.

Red—Anointing, anger, war, redemption, the blood of Jesus; wisdom; love; Holy Spirit; shame; embarrassment; thievery; stop moving forward.

Orange—Perseverance; stubbornness to God; soulishness; prayer; stability; wholeness; being ripe and ready to harvest; warfare; complete.

Yellow—Thoughts; ways of thinking; fear; cowardice; separation; sin; witchcraft. Can also mean hope; intellectual pride; thoughtfulness; joy; gifts; transitioning to the supernatural; overflow; new beginning.

The Dream Symbol Guide

Green—Peace; conscience; leading of the Holy Spirit; calmness; new birth; springing forth; new life; springtime; growth. Green has a lot of symbolic meaning. Again, as with any symbolic element in a dream, the understanding of this color will come from scripture. We see it used multiple times to represent freshness, newness, growth, peace, and rest. On the negative side, it can represent jealousy, greed, being new to something (greenhorn), sickness; sorrow; envy; pride.

> Green is also a composite color. It is made by mixing blue and yellow. Blue is representative of revelation and communion, and yellow indicates thoughts and intellectualism. The emerald aura that surrounds God's throne speaks of all of these attributes blended together. Green that surrounds God displays His strength, healing capacity, and newness of the ageless God. It also speaks of an understanding of all things, and all thoughts that surround Him.

> Therefore, the total encompassing emerald halo that surrounds the throne of God is the all-encompassing consciousness that is the state of being of God. Interestingly, the third gemstone on the breastplate is emerald. The number three is also associated with the three which is why God's throne is encompassed by an emerald rainbow. *Three* in Hebrew means "to gather, resurrection, balance, equilibrium, pattern, trees, counsel, witness, and strength." New life, sprouting, resurrection, fruitfulness, words of life (counsel), unity, and the foundation of the temple/house are all signified by three. As you can see, both green and three are a revelation of the nature of God.

Purple—Authority; royalty; given authority; false authority; authority taken by force.

> Purple is very straight forward as to what it means in most cases in dreams and in Scripture. When you think of the color purple, you typically think of nobility, kings, and authority, and you are right to do so. In the days of yore, purple was a very rare and difficult color to obtain for clothing. It was produced by gathering certain

sea snails that came from the Mediterranean Sea. The rarity of this dye made the clothing that it stained very valuable and expensive. Thus, mostly nobility and those of great wealth could afford to wear purple linen, not commoners. This is why purple typically represents authority in dreams.

When we read Exodus, we see that the priestly garment had purple woven into it. This indicates that purple is also a color of priestly authority and duty. It notes to us that the priest of the time is almost like a type of royalty in the spiritual realm. Peter confirms this notion by stating, "But you are a chosen people, a royal priesthood, a holy nation, God's special possession, that you may declare the praises of him who called you out of darkness into his wonderful light" (1 Peter 2:9 NIV).

Issachar is the ninth son. The ninth stone on the breastplate of judgment is amethyst, which is purple in color. When Jacob blessed his son Issachar in Genesis 49:14 (NKJV) he said, "Issachar is a strong donkey, lying down between two burdens." Considering what the duty of a priest is, we can also ascertain that purple can represent taking on the burdens of others. Interestingly, the number nine has several meanings that relate to this.

Nine represents judgment (the breastplate of judgment), harvest and fruitfulness (the reward of the work of your hands), the womb (bringing life forth by interceding before God (spiritual growth), duality (good/evil) (being between two burdens: two represents choice), concealment (sacrifices made by priests atoned for sin, covered, concealed sin), truth (Jesus is the High Priest, He is the truth), loving-kindness (priests love God and are supposed to be an epitome of kindness to the people). Jesus is known for His kindness), fruit of the spirit (produced by effectually working in the spirit), turn to look upon/gaze (only priests could stand before God in the altar, now we may stand before Him and look upon Him. We may look upon Jesus, who is the image of God), hour of prayer (priests then and now intercede for others in prayer).

The Dream Symbol Guide

The opposite end of this color would have the inverse meaning in a dream. It can represent false authority, wrong judgment, the fruit of the flesh, Double-mindedness, sin, being unrepentant, indulgence, luxury, serpent, or lying spirit. Determining the context of the dream, meaning what is happening, will help you to determine the appropriate meaning of the color.

Brown—Humility; compassion; humble heart; compromise; lack of compassion; false humility.

Gold—Perfection; purity; glory; idolatry; foundation; going through a refining process; something that is highly valuable; something that is rare; prosperity; harvest;

Silver-Redemption; truth; faith; refinement; grace; legalism; lack of grace; lack of refinement; being changed; idolatry.

Pink—Childlikeness; love; right relationship with God; passion for Jesus; lust; flesh nature; right relationship; right standing with God; love; passion.

Grey—Wisdom; maturity; uncertain; unclear; confusion; honor; weakness; frailty; "wiggle room" in judging a situation.

White—Holiness; purity; virginity; lack of holiness; lack of purity; surrender; false innocence; false holiness; religious spirit; religion; cleanliness; righteousness.

Amber—Purity; holiness; God's glory; God's presence; idolatry; defilement; licentious behavior.

Black—Power; strength; deep mystery; war; death; health; judgment; famine; lack of revelation. Note: In the Bible there are not many, if any, positive connotations of the color black. I associate the color black with the number zero. In original Hebrew there was no number for zero. the closest translation they had was the word *none*, or *no*. *Lamed* and *aleph* are the letters used to spell the Hebrew word *none* (*lo*). When flipped around they are *aleph* and *lamed* (*el*) which is one of the names for God. In this instance, zero is the number indicating the deep hidden things of God. Zero doesn't have its own value by itself, but it helps to increase the value of other numbers. What was once one is now ten, etc. The number zero is a call from God to peer into His deepness and seek out the things that He has hidden. After all, "It is the glory of God to conceal a matter; to search out a matter is the glory of kings" (Proverbs 25:2 NKJV).

> Much in the same manner, black enhances other colors. Adding black to any color changes the shade of the color and creates a new color. Black is needed to add depth and variation of hue. This is very similar to how zero adds to other numbers by increasing their value ten times.

> In the Bible, the color black is used to describe a hard-working person who spends their time in the sun working the vineyards. This would equate to black as representing hard work for the Lord that produces fruit (Song of Songs 1:5). In Zechariah 6, black is associated with a strong horse, thus black can represent power and strength.

> We see in Joseph's blessing from Jacob the characteristics associated with Joseph, and with his future, which gives us more indication of the positive aspects of the color black. It can represent fruitfulness, the prophetic, revelation from heaven, ability to access the deep things of God, and it may represent wealth and prosperity.

> Onyx is the eleventh gem on the breastplate of judgment. The eleventh son is Joseph. The number eleven in Hebrew shares many of the negative aspects of the color black. It can represent being out of order, disorganized, incompleteness, or to be lacking. Eleven can be associated with the prophetic realm or its counterfeit, divination (the realm of witchcraft). Eleven is usually associated with doing what is right in your own eyes, which is living by the flesh. Therefore, it can represent the antichrist spirit.

> Some more negative connotation of black is death, war, emptiness, sin, judgment, mourning, rebellion, and anxiety. You can find a multitude of Bible verses that will give you an idea of black as being negative because it is a color that is typically associated with the enemy of God.

Iridescent—Manifold wisdom of God; diverse sickness and disease.

The Dream Symbol Guide

Scarlet—Cleansing; purification; riches; mocking royalty; corruption of riches.

Crimson—See: *Red*.

Vermillion—New day; sunrise; unrighteousness; lust; rust.

Aquamarine—Holy Spirit; worldliness.

Lavender—Cleanliness; unclean.

Turquoise—The fourth son of Israel and the tribe from which Jesus was born is associated with the color turquoise.

> This color is a mix of blue with a very slight hint of yellow, which makes this dynamic shade of green. Therefore, you can gain an understanding of the color from learning what yellow and blue represent, as well as understanding the Hebrew meaning of the number four. There is a notation of peace and calmness that this color brings, which is associated with the color green. There is a deep revelation hidden in it, and the consciousness of God is represented.
>
> Because this color is associated with Judah, then it can mean reigning, ruling, or authority. *Judah* is derived from the Hebrew word *Yadah,* meaning "to praise, to thank, to confess, or to raise up holy hands." It can also be a play on words for the Hebrew word *Yada*, which means, "to know or to have knowledge of." That correlates with the color yellow, which represents intelligence and way of thinking, or intellectual pride. An interesting factor I discovered is that turquoise is also associated with the color green and the number four. Green represents peace, calmness, new life and growth. To the same extent, the number four in Hebrew represents government, creation, kingdom, a doorway, and a portal to an open heaven. All of these factors apply to the color turquoise.
>
> The negative aspects of this color could represent sickness, sorrow, depression, and anxiety. If someone were to say it was a dark turquoise color, that would indicate that the dream is from the enemy in origin, which insinuates being full of false light or full of darkness. It may also represent coming under judgment.

Directions

North—Going up in life; moving forward; judgment; heaven; warfare; fruitfulness.

East—Law; birth; new hope; new beginning; righteousness; mercy; gate of mercy; Jesus.

South—Sin; temptation; southern part of a nation; religion; flesh nature; coming from the south can be repentance; sin rising.

West—End; death; entering the temple through Jesus blood, the blood of the Lamb; offering; sacrifice; sin.

Right—Ability to do things in the natural; what you were born to do; if you are not right-handed it can represent supernatural things you can do; a seat of favor; strength; power.

Left—Faith; ability to reign in faith; weakness; rejection; left behind.

Back—Things of the past; old issues trying to rise-up.

Front—Future; moving forward; what's to come.

Up—Ascending; elevating in an area of life or spirit.

Down—Descending; sinking in sin; getting humbled.

Food

*F*ood in dreams typically represents spiritual food. It is indicating to the dreamer the type of spiritual nourishment that they are taking in.

Apple—Leadership; fruits of the spirit; temptation.

Avocado—Advocate; Jesus; fruit of the spirit.

Bean—Seeds planted; the covenant with God; stinking fruit.

Bread—Jesus; life; money; Word of God; spiritual nourishment.

Beef/Meat—Doing the will of God in your life; deep things of God; strong mature teachings and lifestyle; strength.

Beer—A place of refreshing; play on words for Hebrew word *beer*, meaning "well"; intoxication; drunkenness.

Beet—Root of authority; the root of authority issues (because of the purple color); spiritual food; feeling beaten down; losing courage. Can also imply getting fed by something or someone with great authority.

Bay Leaves—To believe; to leave the bay; honor; seasoning your spiritual food.

Butter—Flattering; to butter up, or smooth talk; food; Play on words for "better."

Catfish—Independent person you are evangelizing; evangelizing to a witch.

Cherries—Fruit of the spirit; to cherish something; to be cheery; play on words for the name *Sherry*; topping something off (cherry on top); treat; garnishment.

Chips—Pieces of something; a favorite food; spiritually, a snack but not a whole meal; poor spiritual nourishment; a small portion of what God is trying to feed you.

The Dream Symbol Guide

Danish—Person from Denmark; a Danish; a sweet treat from someone; tribe of Dan; something prophetic; something that is offering healing and semi-solid food from the Word of God (cheese is solidified milk; whereas cream cheese is almost solid but not quite).

Doughnuts—Twisting the Word of God; "do-not," as in "do not do this"; food; a sweet treat.

Eggs—Fruitfulness; fertility; about to give birth; something is about to hatch; food; bad teaching; good teachings. A rotten egg is a bad or stinky idea or way of thinking, or a bad egg is a bad person.

Fish—People you need to evangelize; the unsaved; Christians; people.

Fries—Something that has been worn out or fried; fast food; poor spiritual nourishment.

Fruit—Fruit of the spirit; color may indicate what fruit is being spoken of, such as orange would mean perseverance or red, wisdom, etc.

Garlic—Strong odor, can be good or bad based on how it is portrayed in the dream; to exhale; to breathe life. It might represent a weapon against an enemy spirit (vampire folklore); reference fighting with the breath of God.

Grapes—Wrath; repentance; identity; fruitfulness. Crushed grapes means loss of identity.

Greens—See Color: *Green.*

Grits—Having the strength, or grit, to do something; courage; resolve; strength of character; getting a grasp on something (Grit is the term used in England to describe salting and sanding a road in order to create traction).

Ham—Unclean spirit; taking in something that is unclean; spiritual meat; hogging the spotlight; being boisterous or loud; the center of attention.

Hash Brown—Taking in something that is compromising your walk with God; taking something with humility and compassion.

Hot Dog—Unclean food; bad spiritual nourishment; showing off.

The Dream Symbol Guide

Ice Cream—Sweet treat; more solid milk of the Word, not the meat; play on words for "I scream."

Italian Bread—Geographic location; Jesus; Catholic church; a person.

Jerky—Someone being a jerk; following the Word of God in doing something that is difficult, but doing it nonetheless; taking in the Word of God that is hard to chew, but nourishing for the soul; doing something in a stop-and-go manner that produces a jerking motion or reaction.

Ketchup—Adding to something to make it more desirable to others; catching up with someone.

Lobster—See Animal: *Lobster*.

Leek—Bitter root; something needs to be repaired; teaching that won't hold water.

Meatball—Perfectly formed Word of God; walking out the Word of God as a well-rounded lifestyle; someone who is overweight; a fool; someone wanting attention.

Nectarine—Fruit of the spirit; if it is rotten, it is a fruit of the flesh; sweet drink; idolatry.

Omelet—Something is all scrambled up; fear; taking in spiritually-stimulating thoughts.

Pears—Pairs of something; two of something; getting united with something; a fruit of the spirit; appearing to be a certain way.

Pizza—Junk food; a tasty treat that is a conglomerate of many things coming together as a meal: milk, the Word, and the bread of life all uniting to make one meal; the body of Christ; many parts being one.

Reuben—Tribe of Reuben; God has seen your affliction; firstborn; forfeit of rights; protector.

Salad—Fasting; dieting; not getting meat; may represent health issues; love; to leap with joy; to harden.

Toast—Something that is cooked; burnt; when your toast is burnt, it means you have no more options; toasted means to leave behind by a long distance; to be drunk; bread of life.

Venison—Soul; desire for God's will; thirst for the supernatural; spiritual authority; innocence; sacrifice; beautiful words.

Yogurt—To intensify; warfare; spear of strength. Yogurt is not as thin as milk, but it's not solid food yet, so it speaks about the foundations of Christianity.

Miscellaneous

Antichrist—Spirit operating against Christ; end-time false prophet; doing something that goes against God.

Air Force—Spiritual warfare that reaches into the heavenly realms; moves rapidly and is very maneuverable; position in God's army as a spiritual intercessor.

Armies—Spiritual warfare; going to battle; war; difficult times.

Army—Spiritual combatants; armies of the Lord; spiritual warfare.

Babies—Something new that has been born in the spirit. A baby represents something that is already manifested in your life, it's not in the womb anymore being created; a childish person; young person in Christ; immaturity; newborn Christian (born again).

Being Chased—Being chased can indicate that there is something you are avoiding; you are being pursued by some spiritual enemy or person, or that God is pursuing you; may indicate a spiritual warfare dream, or it could be drawing attention to an area of your life that needs to be addressed.

Check—Favor; a promise of a reward; reward for working. It could also mean that you have a "check" or warning about something in the spirit.

Chewing—Processing the Word of God; processing what has been giving to you; thinking about something; chewing the Word of God; hard to chew means something is difficult to receive.

Christmas—Uniting with family; time of the year when something will happen; corporate commercialism; spiritual gifting; giving gifts can represent what you have to offer to others.

Choking—Enemy attack; needing the breath of God in life; unable to perform (such as a person chokes on stage and can't say their lines, or a person chokes and can't win a game); hatred; anger; difficulty accepting what has been presented to you.

Credit Card—Walking in something that you haven't earned yet or don't have; if someone gives you a credit card it can represent being given credit to do something or credit in your favor; accredited to your account.

Crown—Authority; what you think about; reward; signifying your royalty as a son of God; false authority.

Demons—Demonic forces attacking you; habits in life; demons. The type of demon depends on what was happening in the dream (context).

Diving—Leap of faith; diving into something; falling away.

Dreams of Dreams (dreaming in a dream)—This is God's way of telling you that you need to pay attention; this is important.

Driving—Where you are headed in life; the direction of your life; what is driving you to your next destination; who is taking you where you do or don't want to go.

Echo—Something that is being said many times; a reminder of things that have been said or done; something that is reverberating in the spirit.

Exams/Tests—Undergoing a test in life; God is testing you; undergoing scrutiny; a trial in life; life test.

Field—Field of expertise; where you work; evangelism; doing the work of God; people.

Fire—Holy Spirit; consuming something; testing; issues arising; hell; judgment; something is burning to the ground; issues destroying things; people starting gossip; enflaming words; cursing.

Flying—Ability to overcome an obstacle; reaching new heights in the spirit; moving past a difficult situation; lucid dreaming.

Fruit Trees—Fruit of the spirit; leaders who are producing good fruit.

Gate—Spiritual authority; gateway or access point into a person's life; Jesus.

The Dream Symbol Guide

Gifts—Things given to you; gifts of the spirit; something that is offered you or you offer to others; pure and perfect gifts from God.

Gravity Shifting—Things changing for or against your favor; the weightiness of an issue; things that are holding you down.

Key—Spiritual authority; wisdom; understanding; keys to accomplish something; what is allowing access to open doors in your life; Jesus.

Kingdom—The kingdom of God; the kingdom of the enemy; what you have built up around you; heart (mind, will, and emotions); heart issues.

Kissing—Coming into agreement; covenant; familiarity; seduction; betrayal.

Ladder—Jacob's ladder; access to heaven; Jesus; ascending or descending in the spirit; corporate ladder.

Make-Up—Altering how you appear to others; a facade; forgiving someone; preparing for something; getting ready.

Marker—Things to take note of; a marker; something that grabs your attention; "point in time" reference to the book of Mark.

Microphone—Being heard; influence over others; temporary authority to speak over others; your voice is being amplified to reach others.

Microwave—Working quickly; things are happening fast; convenience; being impatient.

Mirror—How you see yourself; how you present yourself; identity; vanity; how people see you; making corrections or improvements to yourself; self-image.

Miscarriage-Things in life which ended before they were brought to term; loss of something (good or bad) before you saw it in your life.

Money—Favor; provision; wickedness; greed; spiritual blessing.

Mob—False accusation; mob mentality; going with the crowd; being unsettled in the spirit.

Naked—Exposure; transparency; complete openness; vulnerability; allowing people to see the real you or what's beneath your external appearance.

Nest—Things that have settled in your life; home; unclean thing; spirits that are residing in your home, or family.

Navy— Prophetic; the "See" section of God's army; operating in the spirit of God in spiritual warfare.

Pregnancy—About to bring forth something new into this world; new ministry coming; something being born to you. It can indicate something in your life that is being created by God that has not yet been seen, but is in the works and will soon come.

Pictures—How you view someone; how to look at something; an image of who a person is to you that doesn't change; pictures capture an event or occurrence and bring up certain memories of times when something happened. When you look at a picture you think about what was going on, it's how you remember the people around you (good or bad).

Rape—Enemy spirit trying to force itself on you; something in your life that you did not give permission to happen; something taking advantage of you; a spirit of lust; perversion; may indicate healing that needs to occur because of abuse.

Rain—God's blessing; cleansing; blessing; refreshing; things that are being poured out into your life, whether good or bad.

Ring—Covenant; what surrounds you; something of value in the spirit; the finger the ring is on shows your gifting and where you will find the most value in what you do (See: Body Parts: *Fingers*).

River—River of life; the river of anointing; Holy Spirit; access to the spirit of God that flows from the throne room.

Recurring Dreams—God is showing you an issue that He has tried to address many times, but hasn't gotten through to you yet. With recurring dreams, it's best to ask God what it is He is saying, what issue needs to

The Dream Symbol Guide

be dealt with, and watch the dreams stop as you adjust those areas in your life.

Running—Moving forward quickly; running your race or walk with God; running from issues; fear.

Soil/Dirt—Things are dirty; mankind; humility; condition of the heart (spiritually: being soiled).

Snow—Refreshing; covering; cold in the spirit; blessing; favor.

Stone—People; building blocks; hardness of heart; stumbling block; Jesus; strength; sin; protection; accusation.

Swimming—Moving in the spirit; operating in the spirit. What you're swimming in will dictate what you are attempting or operating in. Mud would be a difficult situation, molasses would mean slow going, etc.

Television—Indicates a vision in a dream, "tell-a-vision"; flesh desires; what's happening; how things are being viewed.

Traps—Things you are doing to trap someone; devices of the enemy; sin; being caught.

Treading Water—Operating in the spirit; working behind the scenes; taking caution in what you are doing; not moving forward in your goals; trying to keep yourself afloat or keep from sinking.

Trees—Leaders; leadership; people; Jesus; covering; shelter.

Tripping—Falling over yourself; hitting a stumbling block in your walk with God; getting irritated over nothing; enemy attempts to prevent you from walking in God's Word; stumbling.

Umbrella—Covering; protection; something is preventing God's blessing from pouring out on you.

Unicorn—Wild ox or bull spirit; lack of submission; mythological creature; something rare that you will not see often; sent by God.

Vision—Seeing in the spirit; how to perceive things around you; blurred vision is to not be able to see in the spirit clearly.

Water—Spirit of God; refreshing; cleansing; forgiveness of sins; healing.

X-ray—Ability to see through something; seeing past the surface into the heart of an issue; extreme openness; vulnerability.

Numbers

If you want to know what a number means in a dream, a great guidepost is to look up what it means in Hebrew. Another tip is to look at the verse of every chapter that contains the number or numbers. For instance, if you want to know what 23 means, read the 23rd verse of every chapter that has a 23rd verse. That will give you the good and the bad context of the verse. If you want to know what a number such as 2019, 1016, or any combination of numbers, then read the 20th and the 19th verses, or the 10th and the 16th. You may also consider adding the numbers together and finding their meanings as well.

Recurring Numbers and Sequences: Recurring numbers can mean many things. The number 11:11, 1:11, or 1:23 will be best identified by reviewing the meaning of each individual number as well as by looking Bible verses that share these numbers. Eleven is symbolic of transition, end times, and the prophetic, so you may try reading scriptures that will help you identify why you are seeing the pattern. For instance; do an Internet search for "12:34 Bible verse." This will pull up several verses that will indicate the fulfillment of prophecy, discernment of good and evil; disobedience to God, etc. You will also have to hear the Holy Spirit about the issue, and He may tell you the same thing He told me: 12:34 means things are lining up, falling into place, or coming together as planned.

0—In original Hebrew, there was no number for "0." The closest translation they had was the word *none*, or *no*. *Lamed* and *aleph* are the letters the in Hebrew (*lo*), but when flipped around, they are *aleph* and *lamed* (el), which is one of the names of God. In this instance, "0" indicates the deep, hidden things of God. Zero doesn't have its own value as an individual, but it helps to magnify other numbers. What was once 1, is now 10, etc. The number zero is a call from God to peer into

The Dream Symbol Guide

His deepness and seek out the things that He has hidden. After all, "It is the glory of God to conceal a matter; to search out a matter is the glory of kings" (Proverbs 25:2 NIV).

1—Unity; beginning; single; God; creation. *Aleph* in Hebrew is the symbol of the ox; Chief; first; sacrifice; "I will." Can also refer to wisdom; the first spirit of God: God's authority over heaven and earth; pride; haughty eyes; return to God's original design.

2—Difference; oppose; trial and testing; adding to or blessing; multiplication; judge; witness; building; couples; two people; Adam and Eve; house; family; discerning of spirits; the second spirit of God: understanding; established by God.

3—Gather; resurrection (third day); Trinity; pattern; witness; strength (basic structure); ripen; nourish; mature; reward; to pay back; new life; fruitfulness; coming together. The number 3 brings unity to 2 and 1. Can be referring to the third spirit of God: counsel; shedding innocent blood; seeds of discord, or discontent.

4—God's creative works; authority; government; calendar times; seasons. In the creation, on the fourth day God gave stars for telling seasons. Judah, the fourth son, reigned and ruled; the root of Jesse; fullness; completeness; corners of the earth; portal to heaven; doorway; to draw out; judgment; false teachings.

5—Law (Pentateuch); grace; fruitfulness; going out into ministry; five-fold ministry; anointing; prayers; protection; the spirit of God; breath; air; evangelism; running to darkness. Can also indicate trampling holy ones of God; being ruled by flesh, not by God. The fifth spirit of God: power.

6—Man; intimacy with God; lust; wickedness; lawlessness; sacrifice; finished work; beast; antichrist; judgment; the number of men. This letter in Hebrew represents the nail which shows us Jesus sacrificial love. The sixth spirit of God: knowledge.

The Dream Symbol Guide

7. Wholeness; completeness; ripened; perfection; order; stability; rest; war; to arm ("7" in Hebrew represents a plowshare or a sword); discord; strife; destroying a family.

8—Overflow; new beginnings; being filled to overflow; protection; separation; sin; covenant; transitioning into the supernatural realm.

9—Judgement; harvest; finalization; good and evil; duality; repentance; fruits of the spirit; gifts of God; fruitfulness.

10—God's divine order; work; worship; actions; completion of cycles; blessing; power; trials; honest dealings; wicked dealings; pastor.

11—Judgement; end times; disorder; incomplete; lacking; transition; betrayal; bribery; doing what is right in your own eyes.

12—Perfection; order; government; teaching; learning; protection; shepherding.

13—Covenant; love; unity. Manasseh was the 13th son. Can also refer to water; divine or ungodly chaos; being immersed in something; rebellion; destruction; fear and not love.

14—A double portion of 7; Jesus; doubled love; to reproduce; to recreate; to disciple; revelation; increased ability to see in a dark time; multiplication.

15—(555); healing; redemption; grace; the same meaning as 5 but multiplied; fullness; snake; thorn (Hebrew symbol represents thorn); protect; snake.

16—Without any restraint or boundary; outside of time as we know it; numerical value in Hebrew is 70, which is the number of nations; well of water; to see physically and prophetically.

17—Speech; to breathe; scattering.

18—Life; prayer; worship; God bringing new beginnings; worship; sacrifice; devotion.

19—Combination of the meanings of 10 and nine; time; the enemy of God, or imitating spirit; familiar spirit.

20—Adulthood; expectation; maturity; being accountable; worship; leadership.

21—Witchcraft; 21 paths of the enemy; God's rest multiplied in your life; devour; destroy; ponder; coming of age.

22 (400)—Last letter of the Hebrew alphabet, which represents the wholeness of God's Word; doubling of the number 11 (highly prophetic or highly corrupted); seal of God or the mark of the enemy; completion; monument; government and authority; indicates understanding the power of words; building blocks of life; can represent Jesus (the Word of God).

23—God has gathered; to grieve; immorality; stubbornness; complaining; wickedness; idolatry; God; Satan; witchcraft; cursing or blessing; fulfillment of prophecy; family.

24—Priesthood; watchmen; heavenly government; divine order; worship; walking in God's precepts.

25—Strength and power; season of ministry training.

26—Revelation of the heart of God; "YHVH" equals 26; God began the creation of man in the 26th verse of Genesis; it is a multiple of 13, meaning double covenant, love, and unity; oneness.

27—To gather; resurrect; seeds; trees; fruit; counsel; dry land; chaos adverted; first fruits; harmony and balance; things that are hidden and then revealed.

28—See Numbers: *4* and *7*.

29—Accountability; fruitfulness; judgment; multiplication.

30—Going into ministry; time of mourning; God ordained; blessing; cursing; rebellion; obedience; children of God or the enemy; blessing and increase; intimacy; forgiveness; unforgiveness.

31—Life and death; worship; indignation; rebellion; authority; operating in authority and not fear; operating out of fear; forgiveness; punishment; lacking faith; the fullness of faith.

32—Compassion; appealing to God; repentance; unrepentance; end of days; rebellion; not walking in God's way; falling away; growth; seeking God.

33—Family; revelation; understanding; opposition; open heaven; rebuke; blessing; fulfillment of ministry; judgement; moving in the spirit; fulfillment of prophecy; reign.

111—God's beloved Son, Jesus.

10,000—Strength; maturity; armies; spiritual warfare.

NOTE: From here on, the rest of the numbers can be any combination of numbers adding up to the number that you have in question. If you are seeing numbers in life that are repeating or random numbers, than I recommend looking at Psalms with those numbers, prophetic verses with those numbers, or doing an in-depth research study on what the numbers mean in Hebrew.

People

*W*hen dealing with people in dreams, it is good to recognize what the person means to you, the proximity they have to you in relationship, and any Bible verses that may include the person and the spiritual significance of what the family members meant in a Hebraic understanding. God chose the Hebrew people, so understanding what things mean to His people will include you, since you are adopted into His family through Jesus. Take note of the names of the family members as well. The meaning of a name can reveal the entire meaning of the dream or the area of life that you are being instructed to pay attention to.

Angel—Messenger spirit; an enemy spirit; someone sent to help you.

Armed Guard—Protection; angel assigned to protect you; enemy spirit protecting something.

Aunt—Someone who is close to your father, like a sister; someone who you consider your spiritual superior. It may not be a Christian, but someone who is older and like family to you; family.

Baby—Something that has been born to you; a new ministry; new life; something new in your life; God has prepared something for you which are now seeing made manifest in your life.

Bank Teller—Someone telling you what you have stored up; a servant helping you save or withdraw spiritual favor, credit, or finances.

Biker—Person who is self-centered; someone who has great power and balance in life; inability to affect others well; moving quickly in the spirit; maneuverability in the spirit.

Bride—Bride of Christ; church; you as a Christian believer; what you have come into covenant with.

The Dream Symbol Guide

Boss—Spiritual authority; reigning and ruling; ruler; boss at work; something that is telling you what to do; authority in your workplace or ministry.

Brother—Christian; brother; a close friend; Jesus. In some cases it could be an angel.

Carpenter—Jesus; angel; someone assigned to help you build something in life; pastor; someone helping you restore broken things.

Chef—Someone who prepares meals for others, or services to feed you spiritually; pastor; evangelist; Holy Spirit; servant; angel.

Child—Child of God; immature Christian; childish behavior; new believer in Christ; something that has been given to you that you have already had for a while.

Christian—Brother in Christ; helper; believer; Christian; the body of Christ.

Cousin—Play on words for "cause," as in what's causing something; a cause; someone who is close to you; family member; friend of a brother in Christ; someone who is like family, but not directly.

Daughter—Spiritual daughter; female Christian; something you have nurtured and raised as your own.

Demon—Things you struggle with; generational curses; tormenting spirits; demons; things that operating against you in life.

Devil—The devil; antichrist spirit; accuser of the brethren; false testimony; false witness; false light; false revelation; false gospel.

Driver—Someone who is taking you somewhere in life; what is driving you in life; lack of control; Holy Spirit; God. It can represent someone you have allowed to take charge of the direction of your life.

Editor—A person making changes; a person who is checking you in the spirit to make sure you are not making mistakes and helping you to correct them; Holy Spirit; God; Jesus; someone trying to make changes in your life or the lives of others.

The Dream Symbol Guide

Electrician—Person supplying power of God; someone helping you get connected to God's power; something that is cutting off the flow God's power in your life or the lives of others.

Engineer—Train conductor; a person who finds solutions to problems; apostolic calling; person navigating people's life; Holy Spirit.

Evangelist—Evangelical calling on life; preacher; person leading people to the Lord; five-fold ministry.

Farmer—God; Jesus; evangelist; a person who harvests crops; maintaining what you have planted. Can refer to growing something in the spirit; taking care of something (animals, land, etc.).

Field Hand—Someone who is working as a hand of God in the ministry or field they were called to; hired hand; worker; servant; service.

Firefighter—Person who puts out fires that have been started by natural events, people, or malfunctions, etc. A firefighter can either be symbolic of someone who is helpful or someone who is extinguishing the flame of God.

Fisherman—Evangelist; evangelism; reaching the lost; drawing the lost back to Christ; someone seeking to get something from you; fishing to find answers or compliments.

Giant—Difficult issues; large problems; giants of the faith; enemy spirits; things you must overcome; rejection; Nephilim spirit; spirit of rejection.

Grandma—Church; generational issue; family history; shared lineage.

Grandpa—God; generational issue; family heritage; shared gifting.

Housekeeper—Keeping your life clean; ministering spirit assigned to help you get your affairs in order.

Homeless Person—Lost; those that need to be saved.

Hunter—A person who is providing for their family; a predatory spirit trying to kill you, people around you, or things around you.

The Dream Symbol Guide

Husband—Christ; God; what you have come into covenant with; what you are in a relationship with; something that you have committed to on a serious and personal level.

In-Laws—Legalistic person; religious spirit; family; dealing with government; family.

Instructor—Person who teaches; giving direction.

Investigator—Seeking into an issue; studying the Word of God; watcher spirit; accuser; someone seeking truth; someone trying to find something to lead to guilt.

Investor—Someone investing in something; putting faith in something.

Jester—Fool; clown; mocking spirit; not taking things seriously; light-hearted spirit.

Jesus—Jesus; could be a false Jesus. Context is important.

Kids—Children of Christ; selfish person; childish people; childlike faith; young believer in Christ.

Lawyer—Legalistic person; someone who loves to argue; accuser of the brethren; Satan; Jesus; advocate; a mediator; Holy Spirit.

Military Personnel—Spiritual warriors; spiritual warfare agents; authority; rank denotes what level of authority you are dealing with.

Mob—Mob mentality; going with the crowd; a sudden outburst of anger; accusation; fear; illegal activity.

Monk—Ministering spirit; religious spirit; humility; isolation; closeness with God; separation from people.

Neighbor—People around you; Christians; unbeliever; people who live near you.

Nephew—Loved one; child of God; family member; brother in Christ you are not very close with, but still have a relationship with.

Paralegal—Working alongside Jesus as an advocate; devil's advocate; coming into agreement with legal requirements; Holy Spirit.

The Dream Symbol Guide

Priest—Jesus; brother in Christ; ministering spirit; person; religious person.

Police—Spiritual authority, good or bad; authority; angels or demons; protection; protector of the people.

Prisoner—Unsaved person; lacking freedom from sin; trapped in something; not redeemed. Dreaming of being imprisoned can show that you are struggling with an issue in life that is making you feel trapped physically or spiritually.

Retention Specialist—Someone attempting to keep you enlisted or locked into service longer; this may be good or bad.

Shepherd—Jesus; pastor; protector of the flock; selflessness.

Servant—Christian; worker of evil; worker of good; Jesus; Holy Spirit; angels; ministering spirits.

Slave—Slave to sin; a slave to righteousness; Christian; giving in to sin; surrendering to Christ; forced to do something against your will.

Transgender—Identity confusion; something that pertains to all genders; social issue; a person who is transgender; transition period for men and women.

Twins—Double anointing; giving birth to something that's twice what you expected; a blessing; trial and testing.

Uncle—Superior in Christ; to give in; submit; like a father to you, but not in a place of supreme authority in your life; good or bad person; not close, but a brother in Christ.

Wizard—Witch; spiritual witchcraft; idolatry; demon; magic; rebellion.

Transportation

Airplanes:

Cessna (small planes)—Reaching heights in the spirit in a personal way; closeness.

Commercial Airliner—Going up in the spirit; ministry reaching high levels; large corporate ministry.

Fighter Jet—Spiritual warfare; quickly ascending above the enemy and taking them on in the heavenly realms; quick moving and powerful prayer ministry; enemy trying to attack from the heavenly realm or from a position above you (possibly from an authority or higher level of attack).

Stealth Plane—Operating in the unseen spirit realm; gathering information; someone is spying on you.

World War ½ Planes—Operating in something that is older, slower, and out of date; doing things in an old manner or fashion.

Ambulance—Holy Spirit; needing emergency aid; wounded in the spirit.

Armored Car—Protection in where you are heading in life; protecting something valuable; strong defenses around your life, ministry, or direction in life.

Battleship—Spiritual warfare; taking a position of prophetic authority and firing at the enemy to bring them down and end their attacks.

Bicycle—Doing something that will require perseverance, strength, and balance; not impactful to others around you; personal ministry.

Boats—Any type of boat typically represents operating in the spirit, as a boat rests on the water. The type of boat (as in size and amount of people it can carry) will dictate the impact that the boat has in the spiritual, natural, or corporate setting.

The Dream Symbol Guide

Bulldozer—God plowing through an issue; tearing up something; smoothing out something that was rough; destruction.

Bullet Train—Rapidly getting to your next destination; rapid movement of God; advancing the Word of God rapidly; training to use your words in a quick and effective manner.

Bus—Ministry; what's taking you from point A to point B; short-term transition to your next destination in life.

Car—What drives you; life; ministry; where you are headed in life. The driver of the car is who can take you someplace, or who is taking you, or who oversees (is in charge of) the direction you are heading in life.

Canoe—Moving in the spirit of God on a personal level; moving in your own strength; play on words for "Can you?"

Camper/ RV—Short term time in life; getting back to the basics; camping out in an area of life too long; camping, as in not moving forward; life; home; ministry; joy with family.

Cruise Ship—Rest; relaxation; ministry; corporate move of the body of Christ; corporate move of God operating in the Holy Spirit.

Dump Truck—Providing supplies to areas in need; carrying away waste; ability to carry great loads; hard work in the spirit.

Electric Car—Moved by the power of God; empowered to get to your destination by the energy of God.

Fishing Boat—Corporate evangelism; evangelism; saving the lost on a large scale.

Fire Truck—Putting fires out, good or bad; ministry to helps people with various situations.

Garbage Truck—Taking away waste; removing things in your life that don't belong; something that is garbage.

Golf Cart—Where you're headed will not last long; not impactful; slow going; will not go for very long.

The Dream Symbol Guide

Helicopter—Maneuverability in the spirit; ability to move quickly in the spirit; *Heli* meaning "son" and *copter* meaning "to go around" (God moving things around you to accomplish His will in a quick and timely manner). Ability to climb to new heights in the spirit and go places that others cannot.

Hot Air Balloon—Going up in the spirit by the spirit; being led where the spirit takes you.

Hoverboard—Overcoming issues; personal ministry that is empowered and requires little personal effort; moving forward in a way that requires balance; not impacting those around you.

Jeep—Ministry; life; ability to go anywhere and do anything; what drives you; where you are headed in life; ability to traverse areas that are not often explored.

Kayak—Moving in the spirit of God; operating in your own strength; going with the flow of God or life.

Limousine—Where you are headed in life with style; materialism; a flashy way of getting to your next destination in life; promotion.

Motorcycle—What's driving you; self-centered; not having a great impact on others; quickly moving and maneuverable; well-balanced life; ability to accomplish things very quickly.

Oil Tanker—Corporate anointing; economy; the oil market; field you are anointed to work in; provisional anointing; large outpouring of the Holy Spirit; corporate consecration.

Rickshaw—Going somewhere that is going to require a lot of human effort to get there, but not your effort. Someone else will intercede to make sure you get to your next destination, but it will cost you.

Riverboat—Corporate (body of Christ by and large) movement of God; operating in the flow of the spirit.

Rocket—Spiritual warfare; reaching new heights in the spirit; going beyond the first heaven and into higher levels with God; Rocking the boat (stirring things up).

The Dream Symbol Guide

Stagecoach—Old way of doing things; difficult journey; rough riding; taking a long time to get where you are heading; acting director; setting the stage to direct or coach someone.

Submarine—Spiritual warfare; operating in the spirit in an unseen way.

Tank—Spiritual warfare; well-fortified; strength; a person is tank means they are strong and unstoppable.

Tractor Trailer—Ability to carry heavy loads of others; deliverance ministry; a powerful force in God; transporting great quantities of goods; bringing provisions for others.

Train—Need to train; movement of God; single-mindedness.

Warship—Worship; spiritual warfare.

Wheelbarrow—Ability to work with Holy Spirit to accomplish tasks; labor in the spirit; working in your own power; play on words for "we'll borrow."

Yacht—Grand lifestyle; elaborate ministry; moving in the spirit in a grand manner; God supplies; God will give; God apportions.

Zamboni—Cleaning things; smoothing out rough edges; God has shown favor.

Weather

(Includes acts of nature, precipitation)

Avalanche—Things seem to be coming apart; breaking off or away from something; sudden change; sudden shifting; a sudden shift in covering (spiritual covering); feeling overwhelmed.

Blizzard—Something is obstructing your vision of the world around you; covering of God; spiritual blindness because of a storm in your life.

Cloudy—Covering; storm on the way; obstruction of vision; something getting between you and God; protection.

Cold—Spiritually not doing anything; dead; cold weather; not walking with God; ignoring someone; a season of rest as opposed to spring being a season of war.

Drought—Lacking the spirit of God; drought on the land; famine; judgment; desire to seek God to have your spiritual thirst quenched.

Dry—Lacking the spirit of God; needing the Holy Spirit; nothing is happening; no action.

Earthquake—Things are about to be shaken up; tremendous change; labor pains; a sign of things to come; alert to wake up; shaking things up; a sign of the times.

Fog—Spiritual blindness; inability to see; obstruction of vision; the glory of God; uncertainty; cloudiness.

Freezing—No movement; lack of motivation; inability to perform a task that you were supposed to do; not delivering on your word; not walking out a lifestyle for Jesus.

Hail—Judgement; protection from God; wrath; spiritual warfare.

Hurricane—Very large storm that will impact a nation or area in a tremendous way; very large storm created either by the enemy or by God.

Lightning—Power of God; judgment; power; God's decrees; something being highlighted.

Mist—Shortness of life; Holy Spirit; things going wrong; dimness; darkness; the hand of God; judgment; veil; missing something; missing the mark; missing out.

Rain—Refreshing; cleansing; blessing; judgment; restoration; Holy Spirit.

Snow—Covering; grace; refreshing; purity; grace; righteousness.

Storms—Dark storms are from the enemy; light-colored storms are from God; things are about to change; spiritual warfare; storms of life; Judgment; trial; being opposed.

Tornado—Storms (light or dark): light storms: sent from God to demolish or tear down things; Dark storms: sent from the enemy to create distress, take life, and destroy; uprooting issues; stirring up problems.

Wind—Holy Spirit; easily shifted; getting blown around and not being rooted; change; adversity.

About the Authors

Robyn and Brandi Cunningham are the founders of Fireside Grace, which was birthed to help individuals, ministries, and cities live to their full potential through Christ-based discipleship. Using the gifts of the Spirit, they teach truth to bring clarity to the body of Christ on issues that seem confusing in this modern age.

The Cunningham's goal to is to guide the church body by connecting the ethics, values, character, and morals of our ancestors into the present and future generations by creatively bringing the wisdom of the past, the wisdom of the Ancient of Days, and the wisdom of our elders into the present—and bridging the gaps of the generations in between. Together, Robyn and Brandi cover topics such as current issues, dream interpretation, learning how to hear God's voice, anointing, slaying sacred cows, and much more.

Robyn and Brandi are ordained under Michael French with Patria Ministries. They have been involved with various areas of ministry for the last ten years and travel full-time, writing, speaking, and leading worship together. They minister very often to families considering abortion, helping them feel safe and supported enough to choose to parent, with a firm belief in the importance of teaching about the family unit. I am also a dog trainer, and believe that all dogs deserve a chance. The Cunninghams are based out of Oklahoma and have two sons and three dogs.

To contact the Cunninghams, visit www.FiresideGrace.com.